UCLA BASKETBALL

John Wooden, Head Coach

Re: Practice

1. Be dressed, on the floor, and ready for practice on time every day. There is no substitute for industriousness and enthusiasm.

2. Warm up and then work on your weaknesses and shoot some free throws when you take the floor and until organized practice begins.

3. Work hard to improve yourself without having to be forced. Be serious. Have fun without clowning. You develop only by doing your best.

4. No cliques, no complaining, no criticizing, no jealousy, no egotism, no envy, no alibis. Earn the respect of all.

5. Never leave the floor without permission.

6. When a coach blows the whistle, all give him your undivided attention and respond immediately without disconcerting in any manner.

7. Move quickly to get in position to start a new drill.

8. Keep a neat practice appearance with shirt tails in, socks pulled up, and hair cut short.

9. Take excellent care of your equipment and keep your locker neat and orderly.

10. Record your weight in and out every day.

11. Do things the way you have been told and do not have to be told every day. Correct habits are formed only through continued repetition of the perfect model.

12. Be clever, not fancy. Good, clever play brings praise while fancy play brings ridicule and criticism.

13. When group activity is stopped to correct one individual, all pay close attention in order that you will not require the same correction.

14. Condition comes from hard work during practice and proper mental and moral conduct.

15. Poise, confidence, and self-control comes from being prepared.

John Wooden

JOHN WOODEN
1910-2010

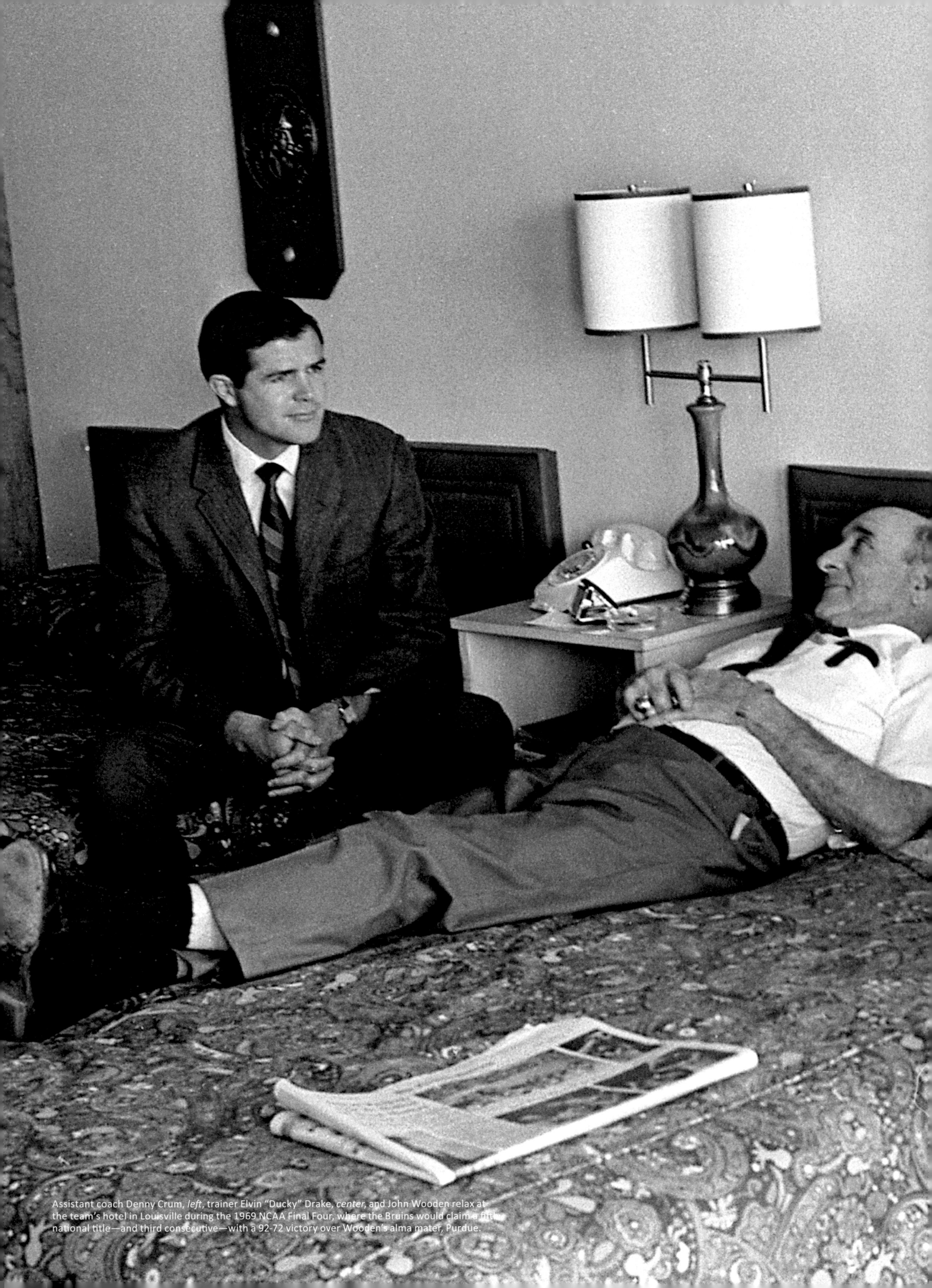

Assistant coach Denny Crum, *left*, trainer Elvin "Ducky" Drake, *center*, and John Wooden relax at the team's hotel in Louisville during the 1969 NCAA Final Four, where the Bruins would claim a fifth national title—and third consecutive—with a 92-72 victory over Wooden's alma mater, Purdue.

Flanked to his left by assistant Gary Cunningham and senior guard Larry Hollyfield, Coach Wooden watches UCLA run away from Indiana in a 1973 Final Four semifinal. The Bruins beat Memphis State 87-66 in the final to complete a second consecutive undefeated season and earn Wooden a ninth NCAA championship.

Only twice in his career did John Wooden receive technical fouls. "I never called officials names, and you never heard me use a word of profanity," he was quoted as saying, noting that one of the calls was undeserved. "The official thought that I said something that somebody behind me said. But I kept it."

As assistant coach Jerry Norman, *left*, surveys the home crowd in Pauley Pavilion, Nell Wooden stops by the Bruin bench to wish her husband good luck prior to UCLA hosting the Oregon Ducks on February 16, 1968.

Most Memorable College Games of John Wooden's College Teams.

Season		Opponent	Score	Note
1974-75	(N.)	Kentucky	92-85	(My last game. 10th NCAA championship)
"	(N.)	Louisville	(O.T.) 75-74	(Well played game by both teams)
1973-74	(N.)	No Car. State	(2 O.T.) 77-80	(Lost lead. NCAA tourney semi final)
1972-73	(@)	Loyola (Chic.)	87-73	(Tied consec. winning streak record of 60)
"	(@)	Notre Dame	82-63	(Broke " " " " at 61)
"	(N)	Memphis State	87-66	(4th undefeated season. No other has over one)
~~1971-72~~	(N)	Florida State	81-76	(3rd " " " " ")
1969-70	(N)	Jacksonville	80-69	(NCAA championship without Alcindor)
1968-69	(N)	Purdue	92-72	(1st to win 3 consec. natl. championships)
1967-68	(N)	Houston	101-69	("Atonement" game.)
1966-67	(N) (N)	Houston Dayton	(69-71) 79-64	+ Astrodome (1st to have more than one undefeated season)
1964-65	(N)	Michigan	91-80	(Tied record of 2 consec. natl. championships)
1963-64	(N)	Duke	98-83	(1st NCAA title + 1st undefeated season)
1962-63	(N)	Ariz. State	(79-93)	(Finest outside shooting I had seen)
1961-62	(N)	Cincinnati	(70-72)	(NCAA semi-final. Very close to title)
1949-50	(N)	Bradley	(59-73)	(NCAA regional - lost a great chance)
1948-49	(@)	Oreg. State	(35-41)	(3rd playoff game at OS for conf. championship)
"	(@)	USC	51-50	Crippled team won 2 from USC on consecutive nights for a conference title my first year at UCLA with a team unanimously picked to finish last
"	(@)	USC	63-55	
1947-48	(N)	Louisville		Lost championship game of NAIA tournament. when I was at Indiana State

Alcindor 67-68-69	Erickson 63-64-65	Lacey 65-66	Norman 50-51-52	
Benton 56-57	Goodrich 63-64-65	McCarter 74-75-76	Sheldrake 49-50-51	Walton 72-73-74
Blackman 60-61-62	Hazzard 62-63-64	McIntosh 64-65-66	Stanich 48-49-50	Warren 66-67-68
Crum 58-59	Hirsch 63-64	Meyers 73-74-75	Trgovich 73-74-75	Wicks 69-70-71
Cunningham 60-61-62	Joeckel 49-50	Naulls 54-55-56	Vallely 69-70	Wilkes 72-73-74

In 1985, John Wooden received the highest honor bestowed by the university, the UCLA Medal, given to those who have made truly extraordinary and distinguished contributions to their professions and to society.

UCLA Chancellor Franklin D. Murphy presents a special citation to John Wooden in 1966 on the occasion of his 500th game as the Bruins coach.

Wooden

Basketball & Beyond

THE OFFICIAL UCLA RETROSPECTIVE

Foreword
DENNY CRUM

Introduction
DICK ENBERG

Written by
RICHARD HOFFER

SKYBOX PRESS, SAN DIEGO • ABRAMS, NEW YORK

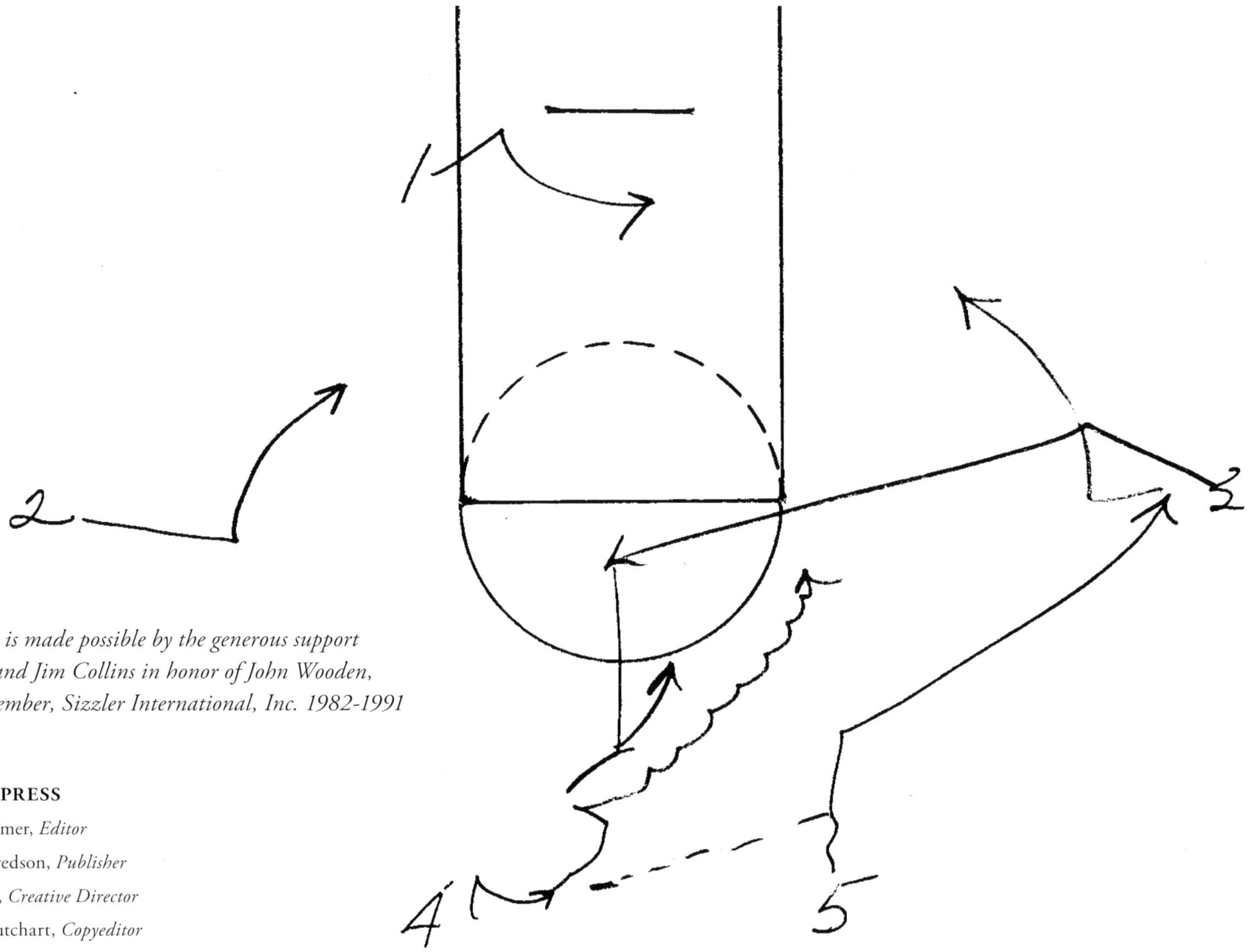

This book is made possible by the generous support of Carol and Jim Collins in honor of John Wooden, Board Member, Sizzler International, Inc. 1982-1991

SKYBOX PRESS

Scott Gummer, *Editor*

Peter Gotfredson, *Publisher*

Nate Beale, *Creative Director*

Mikayla Butchart, *Copyeditor*

UCLA

Mark Harlan, *UCLA Athletics External Relations*

Marc Dellins, *UCLA Athletics Executive Relations*

Bill Bennett, *UCLA Sports Information*

Cynthia Holmes, *Associated Students UCLA Trademarks & Licensing*

Todd Cheney, Don Liebig, *Associated Students UCLA Photography*

Ari Baron, *Associated Students UCLA Creative Development*

UCLA and Skybox Press wish to thank the family of John R. Wooden, UCLA Chancellor Gene Block, UCLA Athletics Director Dan Guerrero, Associated Students UCLA Executive Director Robert Williams, Associated Students UCLA Licensing Assistant Gloria Flowers, Associated Students UCLA Store Director Neil Yamaguchi, the National Collegiate Athletic Association, Andrew Lawrence, Dean McCausland, and Carol and Jim Collins

Cataloging-in-Publication Data has been applied for and may be obtained from the Library of Congress.

ISBN 978-1-4197-0114-6

10 9 8 7 6 5 4 3 2 1

For information about special discounts for customized, branded, corporate, or bulk purchases, please contact Skybox Press via e-mail on info@skyboxpress.com

Published by Skybox Press, an imprint of Luxury Custom Publishing
Distributed in North America by Abrams, an imprint of ABRAMS

3920 Conde Street
San Diego, CA 92110
www.skyboxpress.com

THE ART OF BOOKS SINCE 1949
115 West 18th Street
New York, NY 10011
www.abramsbooks.com

CONTENTS

FOREWORD

Denny Crum

John Wooden meant so much to me, as he did to so many others. He was my coach, my mentor, my brother, my father—my comrade in coaching. I was fortunate to both play for him and also coach with him. I had the best of both worlds.

If you asked Coach what he did for a living, he would say he was a teacher. Not a basketball coach, but a teacher. Every morning we would spend an hour and a half going over the practice from the day before—what to change, what to keep, how to prepare for the next practice. That's when he was at his best: planning, organizing, and teaching. He was such a perfectionist, and his attention to detail was genius. He never wanted to overlook anything.

Coach knew his strengths and weaknesses, so he hired assistants with talents that he felt would make the team stronger, and he relied on his assistants for advice and counsel. In practice preparation, I would say to him, "Maybe we should do it this way." But he wouldn't say yes or no; instead he would look at me and say, "Please explain your idea to me." I would then explain, and Coach would say, "OK, we'll try it today, and if it works, we'll leave it in, and if does not, we'll take it out." He never acted as if he knew everything, even though he was a lot smarter than most coaches.

I fondly remember so many occasions when Coach, my fellow assistant Gary Cunningham, and I would walk down to Westwood Village for lunch. We'd go through the back door at the Westwood drug store, where Hollis Johnson ran the lunch counter. We'd sit on milk crates and talk about fishing and a lot of different things that were not basketball-related.

Coach was a special person. He was a genuine, honest, God-fearing man. That's the way he lived his life. The more you got to know him, the more you respected and loved him. It was such a pleasure to be around him. The lessons I learned from Coach that have stayed with me are about life and how to properly live it. Coach got his teachings and philosophies from his father, and I got those same teachings and philosophies from Coach. Living life the correct way was far more important than basketball.

Before ascending to the head coaching job at Louisville in 1971, Denny Crum was both a player and also an assistant coach for John Wooden, who bested his pupil in this historic 1975 Final Four semifinal.

INTRODUCTION

Dick Enberg

In 1965, Channel 5 in Los Angeles hired me as their sports director. At that time I was a college professor and assistant baseball coach at Cal State Northridge; I had been filling in on weekend sportscasts, and I'd followed UCLA and watched Coach Wooden as the Bruins won those first two NCAA championships in 1964 and 1965. Shortly after I joined the station, the good news came that we had acquired the rights to televise UCLA basketball.

John Wooden was already one of the biggest names in sports—not only in Los Angeles, but also in the country. My first impression upon meeting him was that he was a man who possessed greatness. What I came to know is that John Wooden was a man of greatness and of goodness. He had both of those remarkable qualities in the highest form.

I don't believe there was any lightning strike that suddenly turned UCLA from being good into being perennially great. It was a process, in some ways like his Pyramid of Success. He built the program from the foundation up and ultimately achieved the peak, which was winning a national championship. It is the rare opportunity when you have a team good enough to go all the way and win one title, rarer still when you have a coach exceptional enough to sustain success. For nine years I was the solo announcer—there was no second broadcaster or color man—and during those nine years, Wooden's teams won eight more national titles. I rode the wave as Wooden and UCLA gained national exposure. I've said many times that I am thankful that I had the good fortune and the privilege to be at the right place at the right time during the greatest run of championships ever with the greatest coach in history.

While Coach Wooden and I didn't go out to coffee or dinner, I did enjoy access to him, flying and staying in the same hotels as the Bruins. I recall one memorable bus ride from Spokane across the Palouse to Pullman for a game at Washington State. I was sitting in the back when the team manager approached me and said, "Coach Wooden would like you to come up and sit with him." I thought, "Wow! This is going to be a great opportunity. I'm going to get so much material!"

I took the seat next to Coach, fully prepared to gain in-depth perspective into his basketball philosophies and strategies, but before I could ask him a question, he asked me, "Dick, do you like poetry?"

What was I going to say? "Of course, Coach," I answered.

"Do you like Edna St. Vincent Millay?" he asked.

"Absolutely, Coach," I answered.

And for the next two hours, he talked about poetry. He didn't mention basketball once, but that experience provided valuable insights into why he was such a remarkable man. His focus was not winning or losing but doing the best you can, and that included personal growth in areas other than sports. A key to his success, I am convinced, is his having been a complete man—spiritually, physically, mentally, emotionally. His passion for learning and enjoying aspects of life away from basketball were as strong as when he had a whistle around his neck in practice or a program rolled up in his hand during games.

College basketball has changed so much in the time since John Wooden coached. He despised the "me-ism" that happened to his game—and television is to blame, with the barrage of highlights showcasing individual accomplishments. Near the end of his life, Wooden said

Dick Enberg broadcast Bruin games for nine of John Wooden's seasons at UCLA.

Dick Enberg gleans insights from Coach Wooden before a game at Pauley Pavilion.

that he preferred women's basketball because it was a better team game, that women played the game the way he coached it. I think he would have found it more challenging to coach today's athlete, but he knew basketball, and he knew people, and were he working today, I truly believe he'd remain among the game's most successful coaches.

John Wooden's stature continues to grow. The reverence he is afforded has not diminished since his passing, just the opposite. That, to me, defines his greatness. His realm was sport and basketball, but is there any doubt that if he had selected a different profession, he would have been a star in that realm? If there were a Hall of Fame, not for coaches or players (Wooden was the first person elected to the Naismith Memorial Basketball Hall of Fame as both) but rather for teachers, John Wooden would be on the initial ballot, wouldn't he? He was proud of the fact that he was a good teacher, so take away all the wins and the championships and judge the man by his impact in the noble profession of teaching, and John Wooden was a Hall of Famer there as well.

Consider all the noted and accomplished faculty and alumni that have been part of the UCLA life. To this day, if you go around the country and ask people to associate one name with the university, the majority will say "John Wooden." The university has always been great; John Wooden made it famous for greatness. Now, I expect he might scold me for even suggesting

A worker puts the finishing touches on the jump circle before the inaugural game in Pauley Pavilion on November 27, 1965.

that, because he wouldn't want that kind of credit, but the truth of the matter is that the names UCLA and John Wooden will intersect powerfully and inextricably for eternity.

I last saw Coach a couple of months before he passed. We talked mostly about baseball. He loved baseball, and he knew the game—so much so that in the 1960s he was offered the job of manager of the Pittsburgh Pirates. He was happy that I was broadcasting games for the San Diego Padres, and we argued about who we would put in our dream left-handed-hitting outfield. (Coach included his favorite, Stan Musial, along with Babe Ruth and allowed for the inclusion of my idol, Ted Williams.) He was very generous with his time, but after a couple of hours, it became obvious he was tiring. As I started toward the door, Coach called for me to come close and pointed to his forehead. I kissed him on the forehead and told him that I loved him, and he told me he loved me. That image will stay with me forever.

This book is UCLA's tribute to John Wooden, a chronicle of Coach's time on campus beginning with his first season in Westwood in 1948. Many of the images unearthed for this treasury are published here for the very first time. Were he here to see this book, I could see him giving that bashful smile of his and maybe shaking his head as if to say, Aren't there other people you'd rather write a book about?

I can think of no one more deserving.

THE EARLY YEARS

John Wooden with members of the 1955-56 team, *left to right*, junior guard Dick Banton, sophomore forward Ben Rogers, senior guard Morris Taft, senior center Willie Naulls, and senior forward Allen Herring.

UCLA
STAFF
CL
CL

The Early Years

UCLA was not John Wooden's first choice. The basketball facilities in the late '40s were sorely lacking, and so too was the talent. During a spring visit to campus prior to taking the job, Wooden assembled the players for a short practice in the school's little bandbox of a gym and left convinced that his Indiana State team back home could have "named the score" against the woeful Bruins outfit. His was not a solitary opinion, either; prior to the 1948–49 season West Coast media had forecast a last-place finish for UCLA, a perennial doormat in the old Pacific Coast Conference.

Wooden had toiled as a high school coach for 11 years, perfectly content until his enlistment in the navy in 1943. His service, and America's postwar optimism, seemed to have stirred some professional ambition, and he signed on as Indiana State's head coach upon his return. Two highly successful seasons—in only his second there, Wooden led his team to a 29-7 record and the championship game of the National Association of Intercollegiate Basketball tournament—not only stirred further ambitions but also attracted attention. Suddenly the idea of coaching a Big Ten team, perhaps even Purdue where he starred as a diving and dribbling playmaker, was more a possibility than a dream.

Purdue didn't call, but the University of Minnesota did. There was another offer, this one from way out west in Los Angeles, but its appeal to a lifelong midwesterner with a wife and two children was not particularly great. How would Nell, that high school cornet player Wooden had romanced with those pregame winks back at Martinsville, Indiana, all those years ago, ever accept such a move? Well, it wouldn't matter. He had it set up so that Minnesota would call first, at 6 p.m., at which time he would almost certainly accept the offer. UCLA was to call at 7 p.m., when Wooden would just as certainly deliver his polite regrets.

Odd how things work out, though. A fierce snowstorm crippled Minneapolis that night, knocking out phone lines, and the Minnesota school official could not place the call at the assigned time. UCLA called right on schedule. Presented with one option, Wooden said he'd be glad to come coach in Southern California.

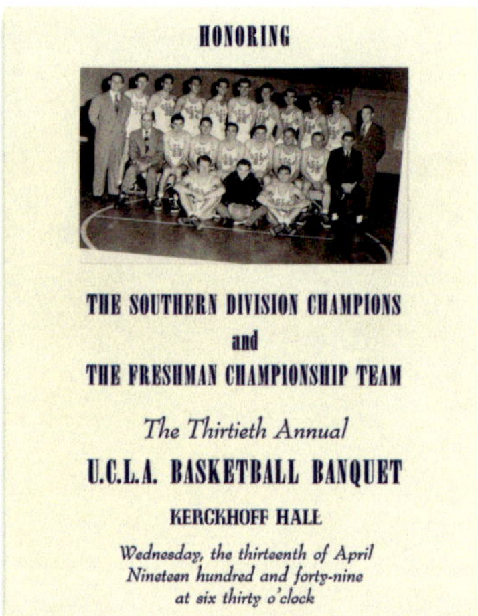

A younger, less experienced coach might have allowed his initial misgivings to bloom into a kind of resignation. For that matter, a lifelong college coach might have looked at this program, which had had just two winning seasons in the previous 17 years, and worked primarily to reduce expectations, both his and the school's. But Wooden, who was 37 when he took the job, had been able to bank a few lessons in his previous obscurity, while he was patiently gaining on glory, unnoticed even as he compiled a pretty impressive 218-42 record at a couple of high schools. Maybe the only way you can survive long enough to truly learn your trade is without the scrutiny or interference of others.

High school coaches never have talent, or never as much as they want. Faced with a similar dearth when he got to UCLA, Wooden simply fell back on that old prep equalizer: conditioning. That was the hallmark of his playing career at Purdue, where Wooden made All-American three years. That was also his coaching hallmark at Dayton High School in Kentucky and at South Bend Central High in Indiana, where he created powerhouses. For that matter, conditioning was Wooden's hallmark in the navy, where he served as a physical trainer of pilots. His UCLA Bruins might not outplay anybody, but they would outwork them. At a spring banquet in 1948, he explained to boosters that "The fast break is my system, and we'll win 50 percent of our games by outrunning the other team in the last five minutes."

There was no reason—there hadn't been for decades—to take a UCLA coach seriously, and certainly not a hayseed who lingered uncertainly at the fringes of public gatherings holding a glass of sarsaparilla. (*Los Angeles Times* columnist Jim Murray once wrote of Wooden,

Before heading to Westwood, Wooden made his mark in the Hoosier State, leading Purdue to the 1932 national title as a player and coaching two seasons at Indiana State.

UCLA played in the Men's Gym until 1955 when it was declared unsafe for crowds of more than 1,300 people, leaving the Bruins without a true home court until Pauley Pavilion opened in 1965.

"You meet him and you're tempted to say, 'All right, what did you do with your pitchfork?'"). But here's what happened: Wooden cajoled a team of largely middling players, who had been whittled down more as survivors than as prospects, into playing fast-break pressure basketball in a conference that was accustomed to walking the ball up and down the court. Wooden's brand of play was so astonishing—what were these fast breaks?—that the Bruins often enjoyed five-on-zero advantages on their end of the court. In Wooden's first season, UCLA went 22-7, not simply a turnaround but the most successful record in school history.

The next season was even better, with UCLA winning its first outright Pacific Coast Conference title and advancing into the NCAA Tournament for the first time in school history. But just as Wooden's two years at Indiana State had drawn sudden attention from Big Ten officials, so now did his two years at UCLA renew their interest. Purdue, his beloved alma mater, sprung an offer on him he simply could not resist: a raise over his $6,000 salary at UCLA, a new car every year, country club membership, a home on campus. Wooden was going to get a perpetually renewing five-year contract that he was free to negotiate yearly. His little West Coast adventure had been fun, but it would be over just as soon as he could get UCLA to release him from the final year of his three-year contract.

Reveling in its unprecedented success, UCLA insisted Wooden fulfill his obligation. He was none too pleased. Irritated was the word he actually used. But, as a man who understood the value of an agreement, he was mostly understanding. He would coach out his contract, not necessarily in a pout but in a steely resolve, then return home to live out his dream in the Big Ten.

What happened to Wooden that next year has happened to millions before and since: He fell in love with California. His children opposed leaving as well. Besides, he had come to be impressed with UCLA and began to realize that if only the school could finance someplace suitable to play, he could recruit an almost limitless array of talent. Even without a real arena, Wooden had access to some of the best players in the country, kids inspired by the rivalries of so many top-notch college programs, as well as a rich community college program to draw from. This, he had to admit, was not a bad place to coach college basketball.

Behind All-America junior guard Walt Hazzard's 16.3 points per game, the 1962-63 Bruins tied for first in the AAWU conference.

Wooden re-upped with UCLA, though he was not coaching a national power by any means. It wasn't until 1962, in his 14th season in Westwood, that his Bruins even made the Final Four—emphasis on Four, which is where UCLA finished. From 1948 to 1963, his Bruins had six 20-win seasons, but in five NCAA Tournament appearances only once did they advance out of the regionals. In Wooden's opinion as many as seven of those teams had championship potential, if not for a "what if" here and there.

That got him thinking, or rather got him thinking more, about success, its definition and how to achieve it. This was a topic he'd been noodling around for many years, even as a high school coach. Wooden was always a meticulous organizer, leaving little to chance or speculation. His practices were detailed to the minute. Every routine was part of a larger picture. His players were amazed and amused that the start of each season began with a treatise on how to put on their socks and tie their shoes (not so silly if inefficiencies here caused blisters that might keep players out of practices and games). So why wouldn't the very notion of success yield its secrets with the same application of rigor?

Consider those first 15 seasons at UCLA, during which the Bruins became a respectable if not quite elite team, an incubation of greatness. In the early 1960s, Wooden, then in his 50s and no longer the wonder boy that is preferred in dynastic tales, was just coming into his own, just now integrating his Pyramid of Success, all those building blocks supporting tiers of self-control and poise, into an empire-to-be.

Probably it couldn't have happened any other way. Without success at UCLA, even short of a championship, Wooden might not have been persuasive enough to lift his homespun homilies like "Be more concerned with your character than your reputation. Character is what you really are; reputation is what you are perceived to be" into the realm of core values and team principles. And who knows for sure if it really mattered, anyway? All we really know is that players arrived, pronounced their coach corny, and passed through his system, only to end up leaving college and living by his every maxim.

All the while, UCLA was climbing that pyramid, step by step, so slowly it seemed that hardly anybody noticed.

BRUINS
55

OPPOSITE: Gary Cunningham played in UCLA's first Final Four in 1962 and later coached the Bruins from 1977 to 1979. TOP: After starring for UCLA in the early '50s, Jerry Norman worked under his college coach from 1959 to 1968 as a Bruin varsity assistant. BOTTOM: A tireless work ethic helped guard Don Johnson, in 1952, become John Wooden's second player to be named All-America.

Failing to prepare is preparing to fail.

Willie Naulls was a three-year starter, All-America in 1956, and set career marks for most points and rebounds.

Wilbur Johns coached UCLA basketball from 1939 to 1948 before becoming athletic director and hiring his successor: John Wooden.

TOP: From 1959 to 1968, varsity assistant coach Jerry Norman provided a recruiting cornerstone for John Wooden's success. BOTTOM: In 1948-49, Wooden's first Bruin squad stunned the Pacific Coast Conference (PCC) and set a school record for wins with 22. OPPOSITE: An All-America basketball player at UCLA in 1950, George Stanich was also a bronze medalist in the high jump at the 1948 Olympics and went on to play pro baseball.

UCLA
73

TOP (l-r): Ed Powell, George Stanich, Gene Williams, Alan Sawyer, Grover Luchsinger, Carl Kraushaar, Ray Alba, Art Alper, Ralph Joeckel, John Wooden. BOTTOM: Jack Zullinger (man.), Eddie Sheldrake, Barry Chasen, Don Seidel, Paul Saunders, John Matulich, Ernie Johnson, Jerry Norman, Bill Putnam.

In his second season in Westwood, John Wooden guided the Bruins to 24 wins, the school's first PCC championship, and first-ever NCAA Tournament berth.

Success is peace of mind which is a direct result of self satisfaction in knowing you did your best to become the best that you are capable of becoming.

REFLECTIONS

Walt Hazzard

This picture brings back memories of perhaps the greatest highlight of my basketball career. Remembering that 1964 championship moment with my coach and teammates still makes me so very happy and proud.

The fact that it was the first UCLA NCAA championship will always make it special. That night in Kansas City launched the dominance of UCLA basketball and the recognition of John Wooden as the greatest coach in college basketball history. But he was so much more than that. As a captain of that underrated team, our 30-game undefeated season was special for me and my teammates because of the cohesion, killer instinct, and total team play that we achieved. Although undersized, we executed our press and offense at such a high level we eventually overwhelmed every opponent.

What I remember most were our practices and the precision of how they were run. Coach Wooden was always attentive to the details of our fundamental skills and teaching us how to play unselfishly and as one unit. We knew when we went into a game we were better conditioned, prepared, and focused. We also knew that our mission was to do our best, to play up to our standards, to play as a team at our highest level. As the streak wore on, I don't remember worrying about losing; it was more about playing to our full potential. That's what Coach taught us, and that's how he prepared us for basketball and life.

John Wooden was above all a teacher. I was so lucky to have found him because he reiterated the lessons from my parents and reinforced their values of friendship, selflessness, commitment, hard work, preparation, and loyalty. He was my mentor and friend, and I think of him and miss him everyday.

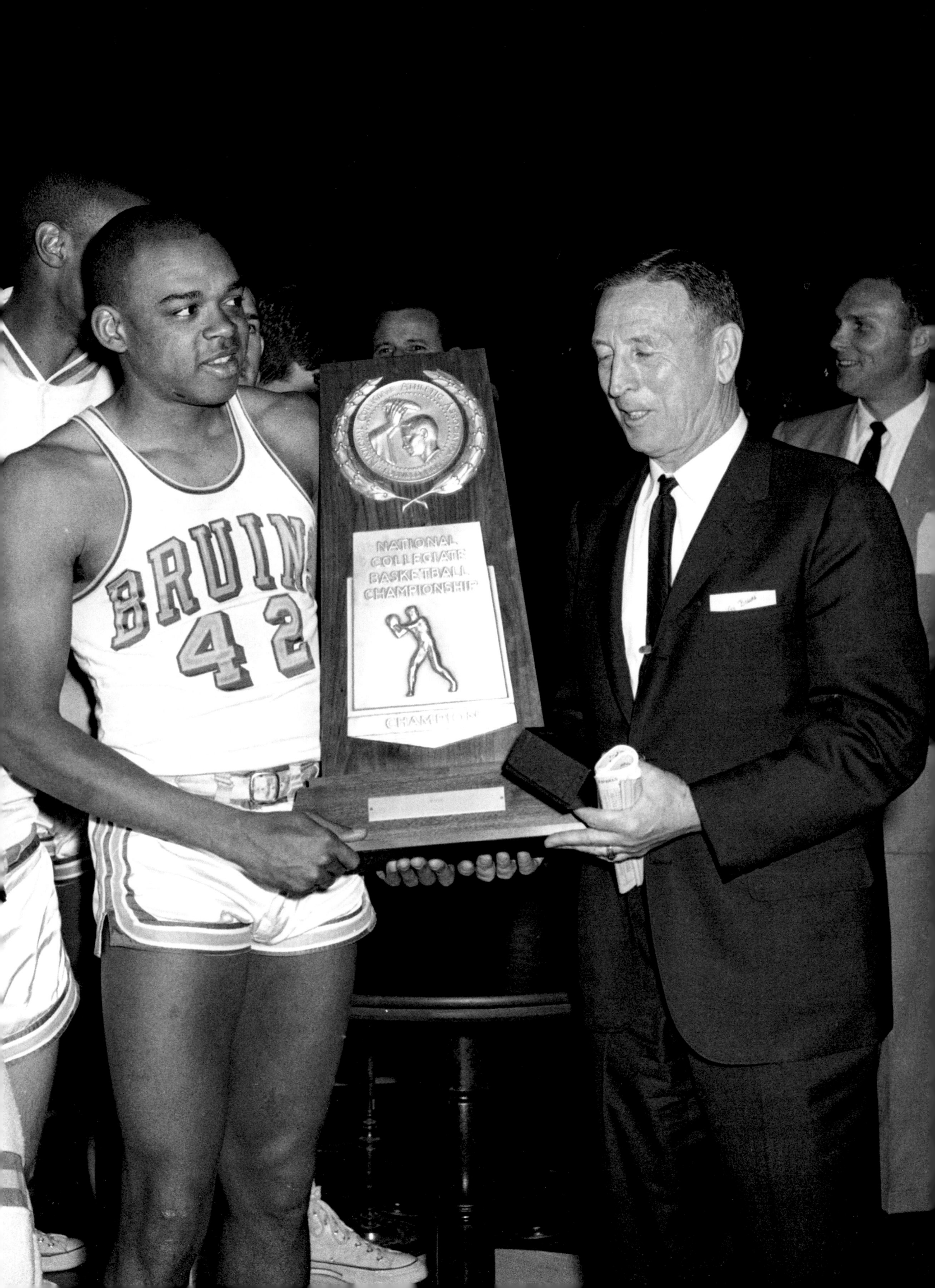
NATIONAL
COLLEGIATE
BASKETBALL
CHAMPIONSHIP
42

The relentlessness and heads-up play of senior Gary Cunningham proved a winning combination during the Bruins first-ever Final Four run in 1962.

John Green, who led the 1961-62 Bruins in scoring with 19.3 points per game, poured in 27 against Cincinnati in the NCAA semifinals, but it wasn't enough to upset the reigning champion Bearcats.

OPPOSITE: Team captain in 1951, Eddie Sheldrake started for the Bruins at guard and forward and made All-Conference as a senior. TOP: Coach Wooden's quick and impressive turnaround of the UCLA program drew increasing media attention that helped build the Bruins into a national brand. BOTTOM: The Bruins won the 1951-52 PCC title and appeared in the NCAA Tournament for the second time in four seasons under John Wooden.

John Wooden's stellar playing career at Purdue, which included three All-America nods and a national title in 1932, earned him induction into the Naismith Memorial Basketball Hall of Fame in 1960.

UCLA
22
UCLA
25
STATE
23
STATE

OPPOSITE: Senior All-America guard Walt Torrence (22) started for the 1958-59 Bruins alongside senior forward Rafer Johnson (25), who won an Olympic silver medal in 1956 and gold in 1960 in the decathlon. ABOVE: John Green averaged 14.2 points and 5.6 rebounds at UCLA then went on to be selected by the Los Angeles Lakers in the third round of the 1962 NBA draft.

John Wooden presents Fred Slaughter and his victorious Bruin teammates with handshakes and medals after beating Colorado State in the 1962 Los Angeles Classic.

UCLA

Jerry Norman was inducted into the UCLA Athletics Hall of Fame in 1986.

A three-year starter in the '50s who finished his career as UCLA's all-time leading scorer, Ron Livingston was also a standout on the school's tennis team, winning a 1954 NCAA title in doubles.

TOP: The 1955-56 Bruins were the first team to go undefeated in conference in 30 years. BOTTOM: A navy lieutenant during World War II, John Wooden was as devoted to his country as he was to his wife, Nell, his son, James, and his daughter, Nancy. OPPOSITE: In his first 15 years at UCLA, Wooden won 20 or more games six times, captured five conference titles, and guided the Bruins to five NCAA berths, including the school's first-ever Final Four in 1962.

The towering tandem of brothers Denny, *left*, and Kent Miller played for John Wooden in the late '50s.

UCLA
32
UCLA
STAFF

REFLECTIONS

Jerry Norman

Whenever I see this picture of my wife and me with Nell and John Wooden, it always brings back so many great memories of the 1964 team.

They did not have size, but they were very, very talented, unique, and captivating. If you look in the encyclopedia under the word exciting, there should be a picture of that team. They achieved a way of winning no other team ever has. Their style of play was unprecedented in the history of college basketball. They were undefeated and ranked No. 1 in the country going into the national championship game against Duke—but were underdogs because of their lack of height. Duke had two All-Americans and two talented six-feet-ten-inch players.

We beat Duke by 15 points, 98–83, and won UCLA's first basketball national championship.

This team created so many unbelievable memories that will be with us forever. Their achievements were the cornerstone for the future success of the UCLA basketball program.

WE'RE #1 U.C.L.A.
WE'RE #1 U.C.L.A

John Wooden reflects on a 19-10 season and PCC Southern Division title in his address at the year-end banquet in 1951.

Happiness begins where selfishness ends.

TOP: Ed Powell, *left*, and Bill Putnam, *right*, served as Coach Wooden's co-varsity assistants during his first three seasons at UCLA. BOTTOM: The 1961-62 Bruins returned to the NCAA Tournament after a five-year absence and advanced to the Final Four for the first time in school history.

The first four-year starters in school history, Don Bragg, *top*, and teammate John Moore, *bottom*, both earned All-America distinction in 1955.

Denny Crum transferred to UCLA from nearby Pierce Junior College in 1957, earning recognition as outstanding new varsity player in his first season and most improved player in his last. Crum served as John Wooden's top assistant coach from 1968 to 1971 before taking the top job at Louisville.

The 1962-63 team failed to advance past the NCAA Regionals, but the Bruins would bounce back in a big way the following year.

BRUINS 32
BRUINS 34
BRUINS
BRUINS 43
UCLA STAFF
BRUINS 45
BRUINS 24
BRUINS 25
UCLA STAFF

THE CHAMPIONSHIP YEARS

Left to right, sophomore forward Gary Franklin, junior center Swen Nater, and sophomore guard Tommy Curtis exult in UCLA's 81-76 win over Florida State in the 1972 NCAA championship game.

CLA
21
22

The Championship Years

The difference between a program that regularly wins 20 games a season and one that wins national championships is both small and mysterious. John Wooden found himself puzzling more and more over that little discrepancy as the years went by. Fifteen seasons in, he had elevated a forgettable program into a West Coast phenomenon, though he had not created anything close to a national powerhouse. What was that missing ingredient, what factor had he overlooked, what quality had he failed to inspire?

It nagged him. He had long worked according to the principle that success yielded to organization. As an old English teacher, he felt he could practically parse greatness. But his highly orchestrated practices, his meticulous game plans, his fine-tuned philosophies seemed to carry his team only so far, no further.

Of course, any number of conditions can be responsible for a gap in glory. For a number of years, that condition was Bill Russell; the University of San Francisco had him, UCLA did not, and the Bruins, unable to escape Russell's gravitational pull, simply couldn't penetrate the national rankings. Even so, Wooden felt he had coached a number of teams that were championship caliber but had ultimately and inevitably faded down the stretch, a surprising failure of potential for a team that was built on conditioning.

The Bruins moved into the Athletic Association of Western Universities Conference in 1959–60, and UCLA responded with its worst record under Wooden, a mere 14-12, not even a sniff of tournament play. Wooden began to reevaluate his entire protocol, going through every statistic he could gather. One thing that struck him was that he wasn't doing a very good job of spelling his starters, leading to tournament-time fatigue. Another possibility was that he wasn't doing much to integrate substitutes into his lineups. The starting fives were getting all his attention, to the point that even his sixth and seventh men in were getting very little practice time with the first unit. Perhaps there was an important lack of chemistry late in the game, when a starter might be out with foul trouble.

Ticket image courtesy of www.ThatsMyTicket.com

Wooden was notoriously strict, rigid even. His teams wore jackets and ties to public functions, and he had a difficult time relaxing his farm-boy standards. But he wasn't so set in his ways that he wouldn't subject even his own beliefs to occasional reconsideration. Maybe it was time for an overhaul.

He resolved, beginning in 1960, to develop more cohesion, and it seemed to pay off immediately, his program once more on the upswing. But, still, even as UCLA returned to the top in the West—finishing atop the conference twice in the next three seasons—the Bruins ended shy of national recognition. "Maybe it just took me a long time to mature as a coach," Wooden later wrote. Or maybe it was the full-court zone press he had instituted the year before, a tenacious defense that he had abandoned back at Indiana State. Once he deployed it at UCLA, he was amazed to see his team, nicknamed the Glue Factory for their ability to stick to opponents, begin destroying other teams. Though that team once again didn't survive the NCAA Regional, Wooden was newly encouraged about UCLA's prospects, with the Glue Factory returning for the 1963–64 season.

And what a season! None of Wooden's starters was taller than 6'5", but they were all fast, all brash. Walt Hazzard and Gail Goodrich were particularly gifted, but they were well supported in this new kind of defensive harassment by Fred Slaughter, Jack Hirsch, and Keith Erickson. Using that press, perhaps the first real change in college basketball in decades, that slashing bunch more than transcended their previous high-level competency, going undefeated with a record of 30-0 and winning UCLA's first NCAA men's basketball national championship.

That first title, as it would for any college, announced UCLA as an elite team, a program that could forever more leverage its banner for finer facilities (a new fieldhouse, Pauley Pavilion, was

On January 25, 1973, John Wooden's Bruins beat Loyola of Chicago 87-73, tying the NCAA record of 60 consecutive wins. UCLA would go on to win 88 straight, a mark that still stands.

The Bruin spirit squad touts UCLA's string of titles at the 1971 Final Four.

on its way), better recruits, more exposure. Just making that final jump ensured the program's legacy, giving it a permanent credibility. UCLA joined that small club of schools and coaches who solved that elusive mystery, who somehow closed that glory gap.

And then UCLA did it again.

Only a handful of teams had ever won back-to-back championships, the problem of repeating with an annually revolving roster simply too big to contemplate. National championships were a sort of serendipity, anyway, a confluence of advantages so rare as to be near-miracles. To reproduce this kind of success with an ever-refreshing cast of characters was virtually impossible, and Wooden, like all his peers, was not going to be immune to this collegiate condition.

Three of his five starters from that first championship team would be gone to graduation, but the two remaining, Erickson and Goodrich, proved to be resource enough for Wooden, who continued to tinker with his zone press, his player rotation, and, of course, his recruiting. UCLA did not go undefeated in that 1964–65 season, but the Bruins did become the fifth team ever to go back-to-back in winning the NCAA Tournament. In a way, Wooden had always been a slow starter, carefully amassing his experience, curating it, and then putting it all together for incredible runs of achievement. Two titles in a row, at least at the college level, was just that kind of incredible run.

It was hardly a surprise that UCLA failed to get into the tournament the next year—although the team went 18-8, it couldn't overcome injuries to key players—as even athletics are subject to a regression to the mean. Remember serendipity? Near-miracles? But with the signing of the most highly touted high school basketball player ever, a seven-footer from New York City named Lew Alcindor, UCLA was about to establish a dominance that would make those two championships look like a pregame warm-up.

Alcindor, who would later change his name to Kareem Abdul-Jabbar, very quickly became the game's most dominant player. Wooden completely retooled his game plan, foregoing racehorse basketball to take advantage of his low-post phenomenon; in Alcindor's sophomore season, the Bruins ran the table once more, going undefeated and winning a third national title in four years.

And then UCLA did it seven more times.

As there is nothing with which to compare Wooden's championship string—7 straight, 10 in 12 seasons—it remains difficult to fully appreciate. Because it's not as though Alcindor played center all those years, or that UCLA collected all the great talent thereafter, or that other coaching geniuses weren't similarly at work during that time. Or, for that matter, that the game or even

Dressed for success on UCLA's Janss Steps, 1963-64 starters Gail Goodrich, Keith Erickson, Fred Slaughter, Jack Hirsch, and Walt Hazzard led the Bruins to a perfect 30-0 season.

the country stood pat, patiently enduring an old dinosaur's stranglehold. The most remarkable thing about this run is that Wooden accomplished it with wildly different talent, and in strangely different times, without really changing himself.

Consider Wooden, who had enjoyed absolute authority his entire coaching life, now having to mold athletes whose instinct was more likely to rebel than follow. The farm boy from rural Indiana, who grew up in the Great Depression and who never earned more than $32,500 in salary, was now faced with a generation that had highly materialistic expectations. Wooden wasn't about to change his beliefs and, while tolerant, wasn't going to accommodate any others, not when it came to running a basketball team. It says something about his stern charisma that a political rabble-rouser like Bill Walton, Alcindor's heir as the face of the Bruins and a principal in two championships of the '70s, could somehow find a way to play for Wooden, and play happily.

The charms of alliteration being what they were, it was inevitable that Wooden would become the Wizard of Westwood. He despised the title but was in no position to debate its merits. During that run his teams had win streaks of 47 games (memorably broken in the "Game of the Century" when the Elvin Hayes–led University of Houston beat UCLA in 1968) and 88 games (including two of his four 30-win seasons and three of his NCAA championships, from 1971 to 1974).

This was as sustained a period of excellence as there has ever been in sports, perhaps all the more astonishing for the dignity that attended it. Wooden had no interest in quashing anyone's personality—he certainly wouldn't have recruited a free spirit like Walton if he worried much about contrary beliefs—but he was insistent upon a kind of decorum (no between-the-legs dribbling on his team), an unflappability (rarely a timeout), a poise. He eliminated the desperation that went along with winning (indeed, he never mentioned the word) by culling performance from potential, simply requiring everyone's best.

In a way, what's most remarkable about Wooden's run is that it finally ended. Wooden had demonstrated that he could win in a variety of atmospheres, bending one generation after another toward success. Why couldn't he do it forever?

By 1975 he had become wrung out. He could have continued on, but in the locker room following UCLA's overtime win over Louisville in that year's NCAA semifinals, he impulsively told his team that he was retiring after the championship game two nights later.

And then UCLA did it one more time.

UCLA
32

OPPOSITE: Super sophomore Bill Walton grabs one of his 21 rebounds in UCLA's 96-77 national semifinal victory over Louisville in 1972. TOP: Coach Wooden lends an ear to Fred Hessler, the radio voice of UCLA basketball and football for nearly a quarter century. BOTTOM: Assistant coach Gary Cunningham, *left*, Coach Wooden and athletic director J. D. Morgan huddle prior to UCLA's 61st straight win, an 82-63 blowout at Notre Dame in 1973.

The best way to improve the team is to improve ourself.

A fixture at UCLA games, Nell Wooden revels with her husband following the Bruins historic victory in 1973 over Notre Dame, which set a new NCAA record for consecutive wins with 61.

In a game where success sometimes comes down to good fortune, John Wooden was not above making his own luck. His pregame ritual endured throughout his head coaching career; first he pulled up his socks . . .

. . . then he patted an assistant coach (here, Denny Crum) on the knee . . .

. . . then he would turn to the crowd . . .

Discipline yourself and others won't need to.

. . . to make sure that his wife, Nell, was settled into her seat behind him in the bleachers.

Gail Goodrich and Keith Erickson

The point of this picture, taken at the start of the 1964–65 season, was to have Coach Wooden, Keith Erickson and me, both seniors, scratching our heads and wondering how to fill the shoes of Jack Hirsch, Walt Hazzard, and Fred Slaughter, three senior starters who had graduated after our team had gone 30-0 and won UCLA's first national championship the season before.

We could not replace three players like that, each of whom was instrumental in the success of that first championship team, but in addition to Keith and me, we had Doug McIntosh and Kenny Washington coming back. They were both part of what was essentially a seven-man rotation the year before, plus we were relying on Edgar Lacey, Freddie Goss, and Mike Lynn to make significant contributions.

We began our title defense by losing the first game of the season 110–83 to Illinois. That was a wake-up call.

At the time this photo was taken, we were thinking about filling the shoes of the seniors who had graduated and moved on. But knowing Coach Wooden, he didn't do too much reflecting on the season that had passed, but rather he kept himself focused on the present and in the moment. He did not know how good we were going to be, but he had an idea of how good we could be, and it was his job to figure out how was he going to build a team using the players he had to work with. He knew we were not going to be the same team, so he set his sights on molding us, the group that he had, into a team that could play together and be successful and reach our full potential. And I think he thought that if he could get us to do that, then the rest would take care of itself.

We ultimately did fill those shoes in a sense, losing just one more game that season on our way to defending our national title and winning back-to-back championships.

I look at this photo now, and I see the bigger picture. Those are big shoes to fill—and I don't mean Hirsch, Hazzard, and Slaughter. I look at this, and I ask myself, How could or would anyone ever fill the shoes of Coach John Wooden?

The answer, quite simply, is no one ever can or will.

—Gail Goodrich

I don't remember ever seeing this picture before now. Coach Wooden is obviously thinking "I've lost my three best players, and now I'm stuck with you two short, skinny guys—I'm in big trouble!" I was thinking "What a waste of time to have to take this picture when I could be at the beach!"

This picture was taken after we'd won the school's first NCAA championship. This was the beginning of what became the UCLA dynasty, though no one could have known it at that time.

Coach, being the perfectionist that he was, was preparing for the next season: Who was coming back, who was joining the squad, and how in the world could he follow up a perfect 30-0 season and a national championship?

Gail had his eyes on his senior year, and then life beyond UCLA, in the NBA. Gail was brilliant, always thinking about the next step . . . or two or three. He knew that he would be the leader of the 1965 team and that he had the opportunity to build a great future after the amazing season we had just completed. Gail went on to lead us to another NCAA crown (two titles in three seasons, pretty outstanding in any era), and then he embarked on a truly remarkable 14-year NBA career. His high school, UCLA, and the Los Angeles Lakers all retired his jersey numbers, and to top it all off, he was inducted into the Naismith Memorial Basketball Hall of Fame.

When this picture was taken, I was actually thinking how I was ever going to get a date with that beautiful girl in the Delta Gamma house. At the end of the 1965 season, she and I did have a date, and then a couple more, and we have now been married for 44 years. Talk about blessings—five children and many wonderful memories. We are still going strong, thanks to the Lord!

John Wooden was rightly named the best coach in our country's history by The *Sporting News*, and *Sports Illustrated* declared "There has never been a finer coach in American sports than John Wooden. Nor a finer man."

What a coach and what a man he was! What a joy and honor not only to have played for John Wooden, but also, and even better, to have been his friend for the 45 years that followed.

—Keith Erickson

25
STAFF
HIRSH

OPPOSITE: Coach Wooden tips off the grand opening of Pauley Pavilion on November 27, 1965. TOP: John Wooden with coach Bob Boyd of archrival USC; in 20 head-to-head matchups, Wooden won 18. BOTTOM: UCLA Chancellor Charles E. Young congratulates seniors Larry Farmer (54) and Larry Hollyfield on winning the 1973 NCAA title.

John Wooden makes his last stand during UCLA's 92-85 triumph over Kentucky in the 1975 national title game; it would be his final game on the Bruin bench.

With wife, Nell, at his side in 1972, John Wooden holds his fifth NABC Coach of the Year award.

Lew Alcindor, who later changed his name to Kareem Abdul-Jabbar, suffered an eye injury during a victory at Cal in 1968 and had to sit out the following game at Stanford; still, John Wooden's Bruins found a way to win.

Ability may get you to the top, but it takes character to keep you there.

OPPOSITE: On March 7, 1969, UCLA defeated USC 61-55 in a double overtime thriller in the Los Angeles Memorial Sports Arena, sustaining the Bruins streak of 17 straight victories over the rival Trojans. TOP: The 1968-69 squad delights in a sweet respite from practice to celebrate Coach's 58th birthday. BOTTOM: After scorching Michigan for 42 points in the 1965 NCAA final, Gail Goodrich snipped the net at Portland's Memorial Coliseum.

John Wooden did not focus on wins and losses but rather preached the importance of achieving one's potential.

After years of watching John Wooden conceive and execute plans with military-like precision, assistants Denny Crum, *center,* and Gary Cunningham went on to head coaching posts at Louisville and UCLA, respectively.

TOP: John Wooden bids a final farewell after UCLA defeated Kentucky in the 1975 NCAA championship game for the Bruins record 10th national title.
BOTTOM: Wooden was honored back home in Martinsville, Indiana, where he was joined by his son, James, his daughter, Nancy, and Nell.

Junior center Steve Patterson hoisted a teammate on his shoulders for the ceremonial cutting of the nets after UCLA beat Jacksonville in the 1970 NCAA final.

Kareem Abdul-Jabbar's game-high 34 points in the 1968 NCAA final victory over North Carolina earned the Bruin star center Most Outstanding Player honors.

A notoriously meticulous planner, Coach Wooden charted every minute of his practices and considered himself a teacher first and foremost.

REFLECTIONS

Kareem Abdul-Jabbar

This photo reminds me of all the times I spent with Coach Wooden that had nothing to do with basketball. Even though we are in Pauley Pavilion, the way we are dressed reminds me of the times I would talk with Coach Wooden about some of my dreams and he would relate some of the things that had motivated him in his life. There were a lot of long bus rides that we had to deal with on our road trips, and it was during those times that Coach would get to find out what made each of his players tick, and it was in this way that we learned about each other.

Coach Wooden was a very big fan of poetry. He memorized, and had on the tips of his fingers, many works by his favorite poets, such as Shakespeare, Elizabeth Barrett Browning, Edgar Allan Poe, and, much to my surprise, Langston Hughes. Coach Wooden took great comfort in poetry after his wife, Nell, had passed away. He would often recite Shakespeare's sonnets to his wife when they were courting and during meaningful times during their marriage.

One passion that we both shared was baseball. Toward the end of his life, we would get together in late March or early April and share our thoughts about how the upcoming season would play out. We also had our all-time All-Star teams, and we compared notes on those. Coach Wooden had seen all the great players of the 1930s play in person, and he had an autographed picture of Babe Ruth and Lou Gehrig that he considered one of his prized possessions. Coach Wooden had also watched the Negro League players compete in Indianapolis. One of his favorite players was Josh Gibson, who Coach Wooden thought was as good as any catcher in the major leagues. Bill Dickey, who played for the New York Yankees, was Coach Wooden's favorite catcher in the big leagues. He also believed that Satchel Paige was in a class by himself.

Looking back on those times, I can now see how special they were, but at the time it felt as if I was just making small talk with my coach and my fellow players. The relationships that we established during those times have endured, and, even if I don't see some of the guys on a regular basis, when we do meet up again it takes me right back to my college days, and I find that my interest in them and their lives is still very real.

I never thought those days would end up "the good old days," but there there they are. Thanks for the memories, Coach, and thanks for all the lessons.

John Wooden was dubbed a master of the two-sentence homily, and his clarity of speech was evident in the efficiency with which his teams played.

CL

UCLA Chancellor Charles E. Young welcomes John and Nell Wooden and the triumphant Bruins home after UCLA trounced Purdue 92-72 to win the 1969 NCAA title.

Notre Dame coach Digger Phelps presents John Wooden with the game ball after he led his Bruins to a record 61st straight win against Phelps's Fighting Irish on January 27, 1973.

UCLA
25

OPPOSITE: Senior guard Pete Trgovich works around Kentucky's Jimmy Dan Conner in the 1975 NCAA final. TOP: All-America forward Sidney Wicks takes a breather as Coach Wooden addresses his squad during the 1971 NCAA final in the Astrodome. BOTTOM: A record crowd of 31,765 was on hand in Houston as Curtis Rowe, *left*, and Sidney Wicks led the Bruins to victory over Villanova for title number seven.

A deft ball handler and deadeye shooter, Henry Bibby started on three consecutive NCAA title winners from 1970 to 1972.

A featured player on back-to-back title winners in 1967 and 1968, All-America guard Michael Warren went on to a starring role on the hit '80s TV drama *Hill Street Blues*.

OPPOSITE: In the fall of 1972, Bruin TV broadcaster Dick Enberg solicited John Wooden's reflections as he approached his 25th year at UCLA. TOP: Larry Farmer was a standout player from 1970 to 1973 for UCLA teams that posted a win-loss record of 89-1; he then later coached the Bruins to a 61–23 record from 1981 to 1984. BOTTOM: Athletic director J. D. Morgan, who regularly sat on the team bench during games, coached Bruin tennis teams to six NCAA championships. John Wooden won the first of his 10 titles during Morgan's first year overseeing UCLA athletics.

52
UCLA
25

Crowned champions for a record 10th time, John Wooden wears the victory net after besting Kentucky in the 1975 NCAA final in what would be his last game.

In 1977, two years after sophomore Marques Johnson helped his retiring coach go out a winner, the Bruin star was named the inaugural recipient of the John R. Wooden Award, presented annually to the nation's top player.

Junior forward Larry Farmer, *left*, and senior guard Henry Bibby celebrate the Bruins 1972 NCAA championship after defeating Florida State 81-76 at the Los Angeles Memorial Sports Arena.

You cannot live a perfect day without doing something for another without thought of something in return.

OPPOSITE: John Wooden in Pauley Pavilion, where his Bruins enjoyed a distinct home court advantage; in 151 career games, Wooden only lost twice. TOP: Alongside assistant Gary Cunningham, *left*, and junior guard Bob Webb, John Wooden exhorts the Bruins to a 58th straight win against San Francisco in 1973. BOTTOM: Wooden commemorates his 1,000th game—an 81-48 rout of Pacific—with UCLA athletic trainer Ducky Drake in 1972.

REFLECTIONS

Sidney Wicks

I remember the moment. It was the 1971 NCAA championship game against Villanova in the Houston Astrodome, we had sealed the win, and Coach Wooden took me out at the end of the game. It would be my last game in a UCLA Bruins uniform.

I was a senior; this would be my third consecutive NCAA title and Coach Wooden's fifth. We lost one game that season, to Notre Dame, and then started what would be UCLA's record 88-game win streak. My college years were a magical fantasy ride for me, and not just as a player but also as a student and as a person. But it got off to a bumpy start.

I grew up in LA and went to Hamilton High, less than 10 miles from the UCLA campus. I wanted to go to be a Bruin, but I didn't have the grades, so I had to attend Santa Monica community college for a year. When I did transfer, I was eager to be part of the UCLA experience. I wanted to be a starter. I was impatient. Coach Wooden told me to cool my jets.

He told me to just keep doing exactly what I was doing and everything would work out. I understood that it was up to me to read between the lines, to move forward without resentment or hesitation. He was telling me, in not so many words, "You are a good player, but this is how it has to be." I understood his point that if I pouted or withdrew, it could be negative, but if I trusted him and kept things positive, it would all work out.

Coach Wooden taught me discipline. Once I was late for a pregame dinner, and he sat me on the bench for the whole first half. You played by the rules, or you didn't play, and that was that. He challenged me to do better, both on the court and off. As a senior I made All-America for basketball, and I also earned Academic All-America honors, going on to graduate with a degree in sociology.

I see this moment in my head. I see him standing up, walking toward me, and putting out his hand. I see him smiling as we shake hands. And I remember saying "Thank you." I remember telling him what an honor it was to play for such a great university, with such great teammates and the greatest coach of all time in any sport at any level.

Looking at this picture now, I still feel that way: honored.

John Wooden with athletic director J. D. Morgan following a victory en route to a perfect 30-0 record in 1971-72.

Junior guard Greg Lee dishing the ball during the 1973 NCAA final, which UCLA won in a rout over Memphis State 87-66 to clinch a seventh straight national crown.

Coach Wooden calling a rare timeout; he stressed superior conditioning and introduced the fast break to the West Coast.

TOP: Nell and John Wooden basked in the afterglow of UCLA's 60th straight win in 1973. BOTTOM, *left to right*: Guard Gail Goodrich, swingman Kenny Washington, center Doug McIntosh, forward Keith Erickson, and guard Freddie Goss anchored the 1965 NCAA champions.

UCLA
33
54
UCLA
22
HOUSTON
22
UCLA
53

OPPOSITE: Kareem Abdul-Jabbar corrals one of his game-high 20 rebounds in UCLA's 73-58 win over Houston in the 1967 NCAA semifinals.
ABOVE: Junior forward Keith Wilkes, who would later change his first name to Jamaal, led a 1973 Bruin win over the Fighting Irish of Notre Dame for UCLA's record-setting 61st consecutive victory.

Much can be accomplished by teamwork when no one is concerned about who gets the credit.

TOP: Coach Wooden and UCLA athletic director J.D. Morgan enjoyed the icing and the cake following Wooden's 500th win as Bruin head coach in March 1971. BOTTOM: Freshman team coach Gary Cunningham (in jacket) and the "Brubabes," the talented class of 1971 that included, *left to right*, Greg Lee, Jamaal Wilkes and Bill Walton.

UCLA senior captain John Vallely contributed 15 points, seven rebounds and five assists in an 80-69 win over Jacksonville in the 1970 NCAA championship game.

John Wooden makes his point during a timeout in the 1971 NCAA championship game; it worked, as UCLA downed Villanova 68-62.

OFFICIAL

John Wooden brought a tireless work ethic to UCLA; in 27 years he missed but one game, in 1972, when a mild heart condition forced him to take a week off. In his absence, assistants Gary Cunningham and Frank Arnold guided the Bruins to a 49th straight win.

Do not permit what you cannot do to interfere with what you can do.

When the NCAA banned the dunk shot following the 1967 season because of him, Kareem Abdul-Jabbar developed an equally devastating weapon: his trademark skyhook.

WE'RE
#1
DROP
DUKE
3
STRAI
Ucla

OPPOSITE: Coach Wooden rallies Bruin fans before the 1964 Final Four, where UCLA capped a perfect 30-0 season and won the program's first national title. TOP: Key to Wooden's success as a coach was not only recruiting talent like Walt Hazzard, Keith Erickson, Fred Slaughter and Doug McIntosh but also making the most of it. BOTTOM: Six-foot-five-inch center Fred Slaughter met the lofty expectations of athletic director J. D. Morgan and Coach Wooden, leading the Bruins to the 1964 NCAA title.

John Wooden and team captain Michael Warren take center stage in Louisville's Freedom Hall, hoisting the 1967 NCAA championship trophy following a 79-64 blowout over Dayton.

Junior guard Lucius Allen led UCLA with 25 points in the "Game of the Century," the first regular season NCAA contest broadcast to a national audience in prime time. Before a record crowd of 52,693 in the Houston Astrodome, the hometown Cougars beat the Bruins 71–69, though the Bruins avenged the loss later that season by blowing out Houston 101–69 in the 1968 Final Four en route to a fourth national title.

REFLECTIONS

Bill Walton

I've got dreams to remember.

In another time's forgotten space, I used to play on a really good basketball team, which happened to be under the calm, soothing supervision of a genteel English teacher. The guy was totally into poetry. He completely changed my life forever.

We called him "Coach," but he was so much more than that. He was everything to us, and he liked it that way. Mostly he was responsible—to and for us.

As I ponder the dizzying possibilities of this revealing black-and-white still photograph, the entire gamut of the spectrum of my life with Coach flows over me like an emotional tidal wave washing away the sediments of the past.

After going down so many roads during the 43 years of his responsibility to and for me, I can still hear the crisp, sharp voice parrying and driving the competition that he lived for and thrived in.

Take your pick, they all fit.

"Now, Bill, see how much better we play when Jamaal shoots all the time?"

"Bill, you would be so much more successful if you cut your hair."

"You didn't really send that letter to Richard Nixon demanding his resignation on my stationary, did you?"

"No, Bill. The cheerleaders cannot come to your hotel room after the game! Or before, either!"

"Bill, I liked you a lot more before you learned how to talk."

"Our fans are the greatest. And that beautiful coed over your left shoulder? She really likes Jamaal. You should try being more like him."

"Goodness, gracious, sakes alive, Bill!"

"I'm not so sure that Jerry Garcia, Bob Dylan, and Neil Young are the right poets for you. Have you considered Tennyson, Longfellow, Shakespeare, or Riley?"

"Bill, you'll never learn what you don't want to know."

"It's the things that you learn after you know it all that count."

"Walton, you're the slowest learner that I've ever had."

There are many terrific things about our Coach, maybe none more so than his unwavering sense of discipline, pride, loyalty, and happiness.

He took care of things so that others wouldn't have to.

Coach was eminently satisfied with his choices in life.

He genuinely cared about how the game of life played out for us.

His truest joy came from the successes of others, particularly when it was accomplished in a structured team environment and when the help given along the way was clearly acknowledged.

Coach's own life was a pure, patient, and constant celebration of what can be.

If only I had known that beyond here lies nothing, maybe I could have made something of my time spent with and the lessons learned from my friend, my teacher, and my "Coach."

After dismissing Jacksonville in the 1970 NCAA final, seniors John Vallely, *left*, and Bill Seibert found themselves looking down from college basketball's summit with John Wooden once again.

UCLA

Hard-charging when he needed to be, John Wooden led the Bruins to a record 38-game NCAA Tournament winning streak from 1964 to 1974.

Junior forward Jamaal Wilkes scored 13 points and grabbed six rebounds in leading the Bruins to a 70-59 victory over Indiana in the 1973 national semifinals.

OPPOSITE: Wooden orchestrated a fifth NCAA title in 1969 behind junior guard John Vallely and senior center Kareem Abdul-Jabbar, who went on to win the inaugural Naismith Trophy honoring the nation's top player. TOP: John Wooden respected referees but was not afraid to point out their shortcomings. BOTTOM: The 1971 Bruins averaged 83.5 points per game while holding opponents to 68.5 and won the school's seventh title in eight years.

Curtis Rowe started on three NCAA national championship teams from 1969 to 1971 before spending eight seasons in the NBA.

Under John Wooden, the Bruins were worth the price of admission for students who camped out for tickets.

Coach Wooden's interests extended far beyond basketball; here, he lends an ear to UCLA alum Ralph Bunche, a political scientist and diplomat and recipient of the 1950 Nobel Peace Prize.

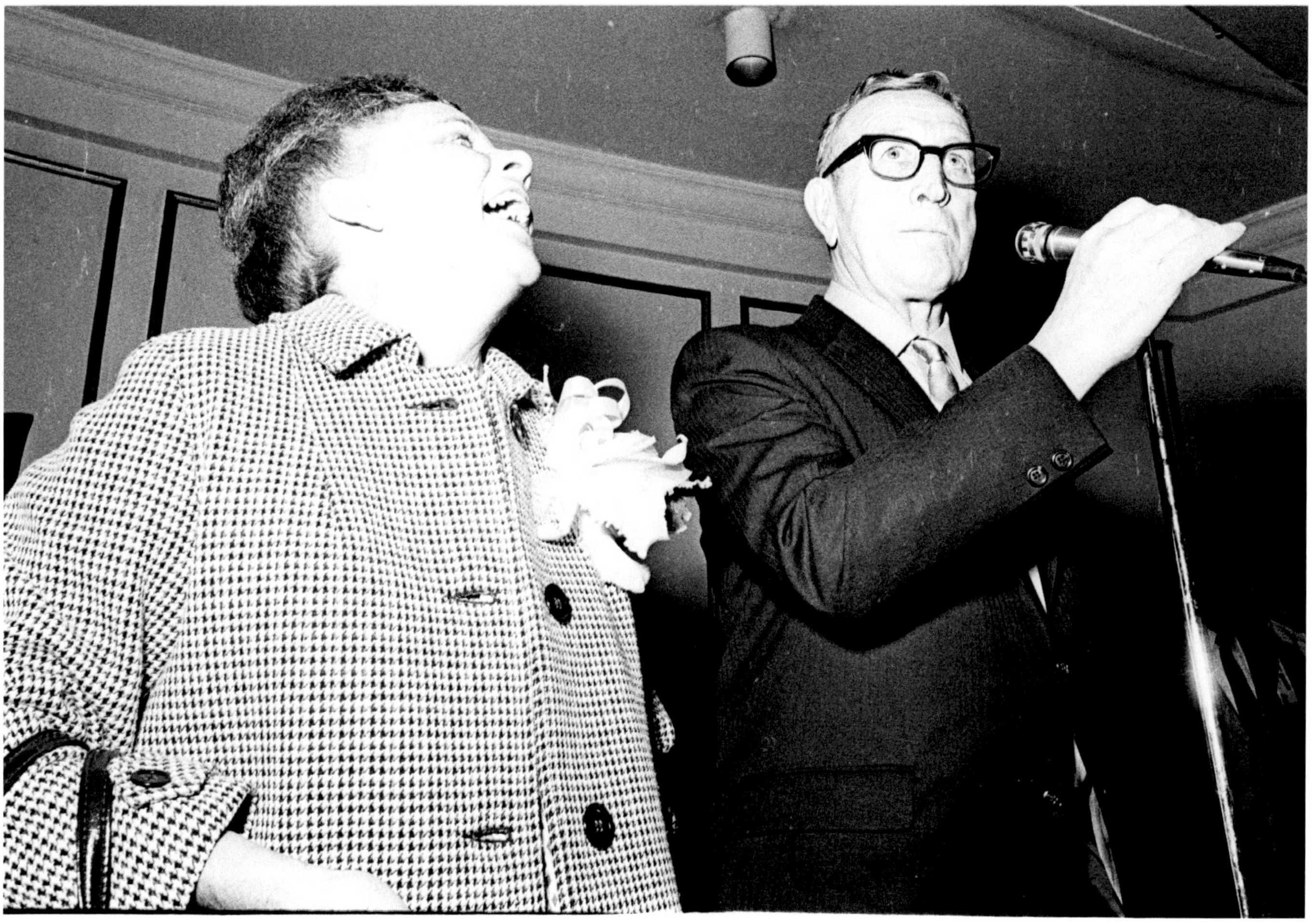

TOP: At the 1970 team banquet, Coach Wooden presents Larry Farmer with the Seymour Armond Award, given to the program's outstanding freshman. BOTTOM: He presented a stoic image to the public, but as wife Nell and those who knew him best would attest, John Wooden had a keen sense of humor.

If we magnified blessings as much as we magnify disappointments, we would all be much happier.

Bruin seniors, *left to right*, Swen Nater, Larry Hollyfield, and Larry Farmer led UCLA to the 1973 NCAA title in St. Louis.

The 1971 NCAA champs had much to cheer about thanks to the stellar contributions of players, *left to right*, senior center Steve Patterson, junior guard Henry Bibby, and sophomore forward/guard Larry Hollyfield.

REFLECTIONS

Gary Cunningham

This photo was taken during a game against Cal, who was always very difficult to play on their home court in Berkeley. I remember how close the fans were to the court; when we would warm up, if the ball went into the stands, we never got it back. We'd start out with six balls and end up with three.

I played for Coach from 1958 through 1962, then, after having played overseas for a couple of years, I came back to UCLA and earned my master's degree before proceeding to work on my doctorate and to teach at UCLA. I often ate breakfast at the student union, and one day I spotted Coach there, so I sat down and we started talking, and he said, "I just lost my freshman basketball coach. How'd you like to help us next year?" That's how I got involved again, just being at the right place at the right time.

My first freshman team included Kareem Abdul-Jabbar, then Lew Alcindor. The varsity was coming off back-to-back national championships and was ranked No. 1 in the nation. We played them in the first game in the new Pauley Pavilion, and we beat them 75–60. That was the last freshman vs. varsity game.

Looking at this picture I am reminded of our friendship and the good working relationship we had. One of the challenges we had from time to time was that we all wanted to talk, but it got straightened out: Coach talked first, and then the assistants could contribute.

Coach had a ritual right before every game. He'd find his wife, Nell, in the stands and give her the OK; that had to happen after he sent the players out onto the floor but before the tip-off, or we just weren't going to win.

When I was with him in his later years, he liked to ask people, "Do you know which coach had the best winning percentage in UCLA history?" Well, it's me—but I made sure to add that the only reason I have that distinction is because I only coached for two years (from 1977 to 1979). Coach had a terrific sense of humor, he was a great needler, but he didn't show that side to the public.

This picture captures the intensity of the game, the love of competing, the satisfaction of winning, but when I look at it now, what it means to me more than anything is the relationship I had with him. He was the teacher, and I was the pupil.

Gary Cunningham studied at the right hand of John Wooden then went on to become the UCLA head coach for two seasons in the late '70s.

John Wooden rarely coached without a program in hand; the February 3, 1973, edition would become a keepsake after UCLA beat rival USC for his 600th career win.

Sophomore guard Greg Lee works past Florida State's Ron Harris in the 1972 national final, an 81-76 win that gave UCLA a perfect 30-0 record and its eighth NCAA crown.

OPPOSITE: Kansas defenders were no match for guard Kenny Booker and the Bruins in the 1971 NCAA semifinal. TOP: *from left*, Gary Franklin, Larry Farmer, Bill Walton, and Vince Carson pass the time en route to another victory during the team's perfect 1972-73 season. BOTTOM: The 1971 Final Four was a family affair for John and Nell Wooden; their son, James, stands behind John, while daughter, Nancy, stands behind Nell.

Wooden's players rarely failed to back him up on a big stage, however following this 1970 pep rally No. 1–ranked UCLA lost a stunner to crosstown rival USC at Pauley Pavilion.

360
bass
260

John Wooden obliges an autograph seeker before the 1971 Final Four.

David Meyers enjoyed a banner year as a senior in 1975: team captain, Bruins leading scorer and rebounder, All-America, and national champion. His sister, Ann, led the UCLA women's basketball team to the national title in 1978.

The 1963-64 Bruins, including, *left to right*, junior forward Rich Levin, sophomore center Doug McIntosh, sophomore guard/forward Kenny Washington, senior guard Mike Huggins, and sophomore center Vaughn Hoffman helped deliver UCLA's first NCAA basketball title.

In 1968, with Coach Wooden and athletic director J. D. Morgan looking on, broadcaster Dick Enberg congratulated Kareem Abdul-Jabbar upon becoming the school's all-time leading scorer.

In 1973, UCLA became the first school to post back-to-back unbeaten seasons.

UCLA
35
UCLA
31
UCLA
30
UCLA
25
UCLA
STAFF
UCL
UCLA
43
UCLA
UCLA

"Goodness gracious, sakes, alive!" was one of Coach Wooden's trademark phrases.

TOP: John Wooden at center court of the new Pauley Pavilion prior to the 1965-66 season. BOTTOM: Wooden was back at center court in the spring of 1973 for a ceremony during halftime of a game against Stanford.

Don't let making a living prevent you from making a life.

TOP: John Wooden meets the press in Portland Memorial Coliseum after his Bruins beat Arizona State in the 1975 NCAA West Region finals.
BOTTOM: Two UCLA all-time greats, Bill Walton and Kareem Abdul-Jabbar, reunited for an alumni game in the summer of 1974.

Coach Wooden strikes a pensive pose in the San Diego Sports Arena during the 1975 Final Four; after the semifinals he announced to his team his decision to retire following the title game.

REFLECTIONS

Andre McCarter

This was taken right after winning the 1975 NCAA title. My expectation and declaration before that game was clear: We would win Coach John Robert Wooden's 10th and final championship! I was anchored and would not—could not—be dissuaded; therefore, I did not cast away my confidence nor yield my imagination to bad reports about the capabilities of our team.

Together, we as a team proclaimed, "Coach is leaving UCLA crowned a 10-time champion." We played the game girded with the shield of confidence against the fiery darts of Kentucky's pressure. I played every minute of the game, guarding that with which I had been entrusted. My feet and my hands were impelled with the preparation of Wooden practices. I scored the last two points to seal both the win and my declaration of 10 NCAA men's basketball national championships for UCLA.

I saluted him with my words saying "Have a good life, Coach." I stood next to a general who wore the reward of confidence around his neck, celebrating being the best we can be. Mission accomplished!

In the 1975 Final Four title game, assistant coaches, *left to right*, Frank Arnold and Gary Cunningham had a ringside seat for John Wooden's swan song and record 10th NCAA title.

TOP: *left to right*, sophomores Wilbert Olinde and Marques Johnson and junior Andre McCarter celebrate UCLA's 92-85 win over Kentucky in the 1975 NCAA championship game. BOTTOM: John Wooden's final Bruin team photo, taken after his last game as the head basketball coach at UCLA.

A window in the mind of the master; John Wooden's 10 NCAA titles in 12 seasons stands among the safest records in sports.

THE GOLDEN YEARS

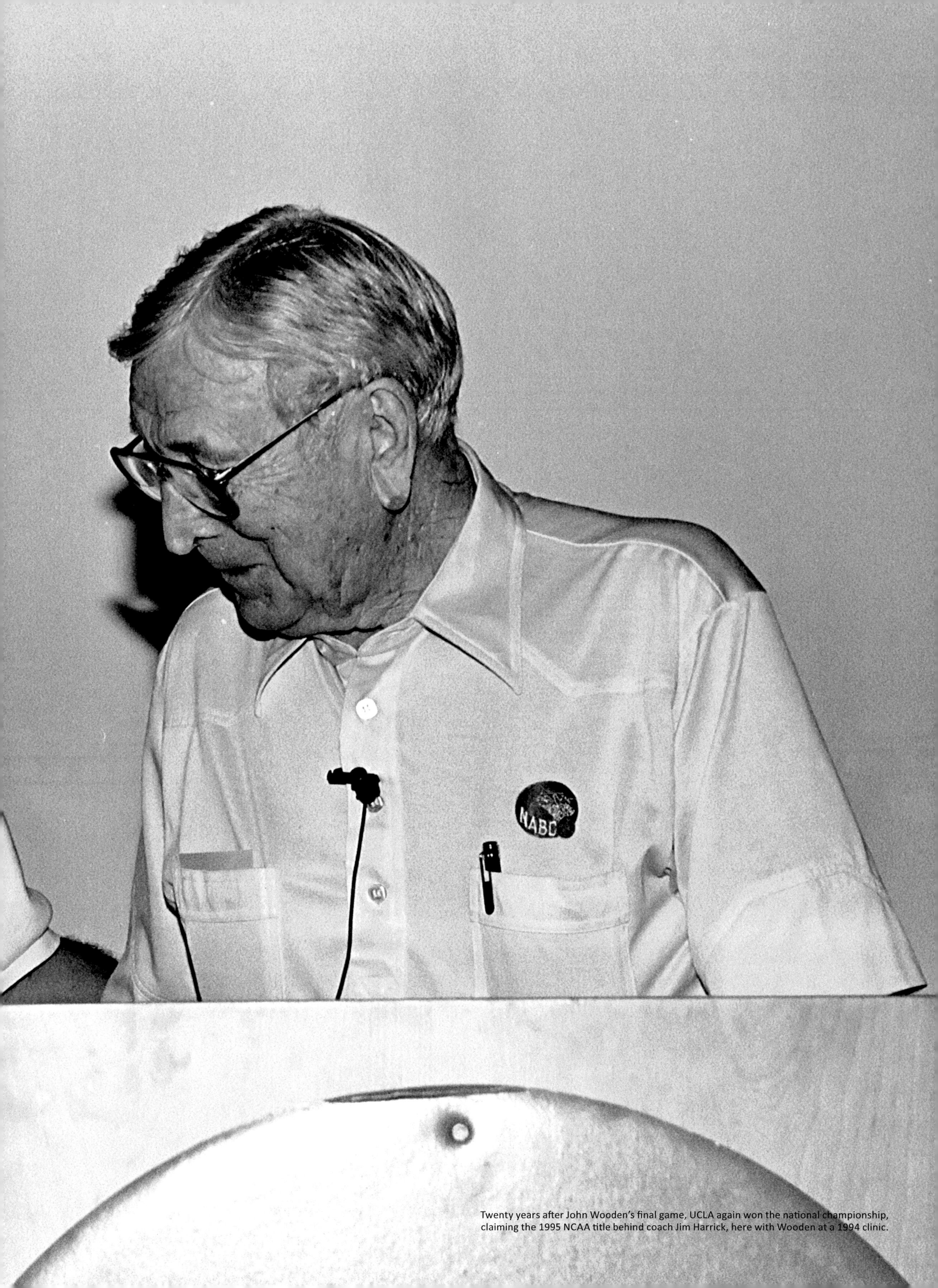

Twenty years after John Wooden's final game, UCLA again won the national championship, claiming the 1995 NCAA title behind coach Jim Harrick, here with Wooden at a 1994 clinic.

The Golden Years

Twenty years would pass before UCLA's men's basketball program again won a national championship. This is not to say the Bruins were not successful; they began most seasons as a contender, often won 20-plus games, and delivered numerous deep runs and exciting moments come March Madness. But the days of fairly automatic league championships ended when John Wooden retired in 1975 after earning a record 10th NCAA championship.

Wooden remained a kind and encouraging presence in the years that followed, cheering on the team with Nell from their seats just behind the UCLA bench. His presence could not deliver championships—what a difference one row makes!—but at least it offered a certain reassurance, a kind of support. Although his position in the community offered him plenty of opportunity, Wooden refused to meddle, his calm itself every successor's tacit endorsement. None of the men who subsequently wore his whistle could entirely enjoy working in Wooden's shadow, but they could enjoy his support.

All of UCLA enjoyed Wooden's support and friendship in retirement, really, a period that lasted much longer than his coaching days and may have been just as meaningful. His allegiance was as natural as his game attendance. He often appeared on campus, to speak to coaches and staff, or for a lecture in a UCLA classroom. The man who rebuffed all offers to coach elsewhere—it was reported that he nixed a high-dollar offer from the Lakers to coach in the NBA—continued to represent his university, the very modesty of his life beyond the campus confirming the values he brought there.

In turn, the school did what it could to honor Wooden, to repay his loyalty. In 1983 UCLA opened the John R. Wooden Recreation and Sports Center, Wooden's only provision for the use of his name being that it be "open to all students and the campus community, not just selected groups," meaning not just athletes. He was a teacher, first and foremost. In 2003 the school also christened the basketball court in his name, but also with a Wooden provision: He wouldn't sanction it unless his wife's name was included, hence the Nell and John Wooden Court. UCLA established the Wooden Academy in 2007 to teach his life and principles, and its school of management began the John Wooden Global Leadership Award in 2008, recognizing his life and principles extended beyond sports.

His name had coast-to-coast cachet, and there were a number of efforts to honor it throughout college basketball. The Wooden Award was established to celebrate the best men's and women's college basketball players. A tournament, the John R. Wooden Classic, was established in his name in 1994, an annual event that benefits one of his favorite charities, Special Olympics Southern California.

Those early years of retirement were rich ones, the accolades piling up on the doorstep of the Woodens' suburban condo. He was regularly inducted into halls of fame (sometimes at their start-up, as if the recognition couldn't wait) and honored by presidents and other civic institutions. He was hardly idle during this time, conducting camps and continuing to spread his gospel in a series of inspirational and motivational books and children's books, too. But more important, he continued to serve as a wellspring of wisdom for his players, who were frequent visitors and constant callers.

It was strange that a man so set in his ways, so insistent upon discipline, so rigid in his beliefs could end up bridging so many generational gaps, his ethos proving more universal than more modern philosophies. Bill Walton, one of his counterculture centers, once challenged him over the right to wear a full beard. Wooden acknowledged the right but reserved his own right as coach of the team. "We're going to miss you," he told a startled Walton. Walton shaved the beard but, more

In retirement, John Wooden shared his wit and wisdom both as an engaging public speaker and also as the author of numerous books.

Kareem Abdul-Jabbar, Walt Hazzard, and Gail Goodrich returned to Pauley Pavilion in June 1987 for *A Salute to John Wooden*.

to the point, maintained a schedule of weekly calls to his old coach, signing off the same way every time by saying "I love you."

Wooden's impact was not confined to his stars—the 17 All-Americans and more than two dozen NBA players who passed through his program—but rather was felt by all, indiscriminately. Wooden maintained ties with almost every one of his players and, at one point, could locate 172 of the 180 Bruins he'd coached. It wasn't just Walton checking in, after all; Swen Nater used to regularly croon "Wind beneath My Wings" to his old, somewhat bemused, coach.

But even Wooden's main mantra, "Make each day your masterpiece," was challenged when Nell, his wife of 53 years—or as he used to say, "my sweetheart of 60"—died in 1985. Although Nell had been a fixture at his side throughout his career, attending coaching conventions and cheering behind his bench during games, nobody could have truly understood the depth of his devotion to her or the extent of their companionship.

Without her, he was bereft, devastated by the loss. Friends and former players of his were concerned at his withdrawal, and not a few chose to remind him of his own well-crafted encouragements, chief among them, "Avoid the peaks and the valleys." But as his grief played out, it was probably more a celebration of the love the two shared than a cause for alarm. It was, in most ways, sweeter than it was sad.

Every month, on the 21st day, in memory of her death, Wooden sat down in the den of his Encino condo, the room Nell had decorated with his 10 championship team pictures, arranged in the signature pyramid, and wrote Nell a love letter. And then he'd put it into an envelope and add it to all the other love letters, all of them neatly bound in a yellow ribbon, placed just as neatly on her pillow. Wooden emerged from the deepest part of his grieving, eventually pulling back the sheets instead of sleeping atop their bed so as to not disturb her side. He had to consider the life around him, even as he had been so absorbed by death. He was surrounded by so much of it, notably 13 great-grandchildren (more even than his NCAA titles), and while he would continue to nurse his grief, he would once more be alert to the possibilities of life. He was, after all, a lifelong teacher, with lifelong responsibilities.

A competitor once observed that John Wooden was a better coach at 55 than he was at 50, and better at 60 than he was at 55. Meaning he was a lifelong learner as well. No small thing for men of unchanging values, set in their ways. He once heard Wilt Chamberlain complain of coaching

Following John Wooden's death on June 4, 2010, his family donated to UCLA the belongings from his den, which has been meticulously recreated and will remain on permanent display in the UCLA Athletics Hall of Fame on campus.

rhetoric that confused players with things: "You handle things," Chamberlain said, "you work with people." That very day, Wooden contacted his publisher and asked that a chapter heading in one of his books that read "Handling Your Players" be replaced by "Working with Your Players."

In time Wooden resumed his role, where he was still needed, as the arbiter of common sense, of decency, of dignity. To the end he refused to capitalize on his name—somebody other than him might have called it a brand—refusing shoe contracts, endorsements, the usual residuals of success. Instead he remained available, freely so, answering mail in his precise cursive, answering calls in his polite twang. It was only in his retirement, when the hurly-burly of the seasons was replaced by the calmness of his leisure , that his lessons seemed to unfold for us, his old puzzlers, like "Be quick, don't hurry," suddenly making sense.

It was his final, most important gift: living his life absolutely consistently, in complete harmony with all those old homilies. He was no saint—ask any referee who ever got an earful from Wooden—but he was no hypocrite either. He had taught sensibility his entire life, whether it was the right way to tie one's shoes or just simple down-to-earth considerations like players picking up after themselves in visitor's locker rooms. And he had lived those lessons, his career sensibility reverberating throughout his retirement.

He lived those lessons for a long time. He told visitors he no longer had a fear of death, not since Nell left, and always gave the impression he was just biding his time until he could join her. In the meantime, he'd just do what he could. But it wasn't for another 25 years that he did join her, on June 4, 2010, at the age of 99, just months shy of the century mark. What a long time to do what he could.

A life lived that long, and that well, inspires more gratitude than it does grief, and his departure was, of all things, heartwarming. It had been a long journey, touching countless lives along the way. Hundreds of former players, fellow coaches, university colleagues, and admirers attended the memorial service held a few weeks after his passing in Pauley Pavilion on the Nell and John Wooden Court. But you wonder if Wooden, the lifelong teacher, wouldn't have been equally gratified by the impromptu gathering that assembled on campus the night of his death.

UCLA students, hundreds of them, hardly any of whom would have had any direct interaction with the man, erupted in the Bruin "Eight-Clap," a trademark cheer introduced in 1948—the year of Wooden's arrival at UCLA—followed by a moment of silence.

TOP: The 1984-85 Bruins gathered for a picture with Coach Wooden and his protégé Walt Hazzard, who, in his first year as UCLA head coach, led the Bruins to victory in the National Invitation Tournament. BOTTOM: Admirers lined up to meet Wooden and get a signed copy of his autobiography, *They Call Me Coach*.

Frank Oliver/Journal & Courier

In honor of his achievements, ESPN declared John Wooden "The Greatest Coach of the 20th Century" and *The Sporting News* proclaimed him "The Greatest Coach of All Time."

In 1980, *left to right*, Kareem Abdul-Jabbar, John Wooden, UCLA Chancellor Charles E. Young, and Los Angeles mayor Tom Bradley herald the building of the John R. Wooden Recreation and Sports Center.

Celebrating
UCLA
20

OPPOSITE: Twenty years after UCLA's Recreation and Sports Center was christened in his honor, the legendary Bruin coach delivered the keynote speech at the Wooden Center Appreciation Day in 2003. ABOVE: Wooden appeared a proud father figure when protégés Kareem Abdul-Jabbar and Bill Walton had their jersey numbers retired during a 1990 halftime ceremony.

OPPOSITE: John Wooden surrounded by family in 1998 with the original Pauley Pavilion jump circle. ABOVE: For years following his retirement, John Wooden conducted summer basketball camps for boys and girls, including his granddaughter, Cathleen, *left*.

UCLA

Susana Meyer
Daniel Meyer
UCLA

If you don't have time to do it right, when will you have time to do it over?

OPPOSITE: John Wooden autographs a ball for a young Bruin fan. TOP: Entertainer Bob Hope congratulates Wooden at his retirement/birthday party in Pauley Pavilion on October 14, 1975. BOTTOM: Joining the Woodens at the party were UCLA athletic director J. D. Morgan, *second from right*, and Los Angeles mayor Tom Bradley, *right*, both Bruin alums who played tennis and competed in track and field, respectively.

REFLECTIONS

Marques Johnson

Looking at this photograph brings a flood of memories to mind. The year is 1977, and I had been chosen as the very first winner of the John R. Wooden Award, which was established by the Los Angeles Athletic Club to honor the most outstanding college basketball player.

I look extremely nervous, while Coach Wooden looks genuinely happy. But words cannot accurately describe the emotions coursing through my being at that very moment.

Coach had retired two seasons past, after my sophomore year when we won his 10th and final NCAA championship. We made it back to the Final Four my junior year, after which I thought seriously about leaving school early and entering the NBA draft. There was interest from teams in both the NBA and the old ABA, but I removed my name from consideration just hours before the NBA draft, which allowed me to keep my eligibility and play my senior season of college basketball. It was not an easy decision. What tilted me toward returning to UCLA was the opportunity to become the first winner of the Wooden Award.

Coach Wooden taught us to play to our potential, and you could say I was driven to be the best that I could be. Heading into my senior year, I worked out on the track in the morning, did sessions in the swimming pool, played full-court games, then worked on my shooting long after dark under the lights on the outdoor courts near my apartment. I even went to UCLA's volleyball coach, Al Scates, to get tips on adding explosion to my leaping ability when the NCAA announced that, after 10 years, it was lifting the ban on the dunk shot. I used that to my advantage, racking up 63 dunks that season.

What I love about the Wooden Award is that it takes into account academics as well as athletics, plus it recognizes achievement both on and off the court. It is about being a complete person and a complete player. Each of the five figures on the trophy represents one of the aspects of the game Coach Wooden held in high regard: shooting, rebounding, passing, dribbling, and defense. I was taught by Coach to work hard, and thanks to the effort I put in, along with the access I had to many of the greatest coaches and athletes and the knowledge I gained from them, I was able to fulfill my dreams.

As a result, my name will forever be linked to the greatest man in the history of college basketball. It gets no better than that.

ANGELES
LAA
THE
N R. WOODEN
UAL AWARD

OPPOSITE: At a luncheon prior to the December 20, 2003, dedication of Nell and John Wooden Court in Pauley Pavilion, the humble coach offered his thoughts and thanks. TOP: Attending the Wooden Center Appreciation Day earlier that year were Wooden's close friends and loyal supporters of UCLA and Bruin Athletics Jim and Carol Collins. BOTTOM: Wooden with Bruin great Ann Meyers Drysdale, the first UCLA women's basketball player inducted into the Naismith Memorial Basketball Hall of Fame.

John Wooden sits with UCLA softball player Jennifer Schroeder and basketball player Kevin Love at the inaugural Wooden Academy, a leadership development program founded in 2007 designed to teach Bruin student-athletes the values and principles that Wooden used to create his Pyramid of Success.

TOP: In his retirement, John Wooden attended countless UCLA events and was a staunch supporter of the Bruin women's gymnastics team, which has enjoyed Woodenesque success by claiming six NCAA team championships. BOTTOM: Kareem Abdul-Jabbar, John Wooden, and Bill Walton autographed the original Pauley Pavilion center jump circle, which was used from 1965 to 1982.

ESPN announcer Dick Vitale visits Coach Wooden in his regular seat in Pauley Pavilion. In a 2010 interview Wooden said, "Dick's presence and personality helps to keep college basketball in the limelight."

It is what you learn after you know it all that counts.

College basketball's elder statesman received numerous prestigious honors in retirement, including the Ronald Reagan Distinguished American Award, the NCAA's Gerald R. Ford Award and Theodore Roosevelt Award, and the U.S. Medal of Freedom.

John Wooden maintained a close relationship with his players, including Kareem Abdul-Jabbar, who said, "He was more like a parent than a coach. We learned all about those aspects of life that most kids want to skip over. He wouldn't let us do that."

Ever humble, John Wooden posed reluctantly for this photograph with the trove of trophies his UCLA teams won.

NATIONAL
COLLEGIATE
BASKETBALL
CHAMPIONSHIP

A capacity crowd turned out for the 2003 dedication of the Nell and John Wooden Court in Pauley Pavilion. Ever the gentleman, he insisted Nell's name come first. The couple met at Martinsville High School in Indiana and was married for 53 years. Nell Wooden passed on March 21, 1985.

REFLECTIONS

Jamaal Wilkes and Michael Warren

It was always a treat to see Coach Wooden, even more so during the last several years of his life. We knew his time was drawing closer with each and every day. The fact that this picture was taken at what would be Coach Wooden's last public appearance makes it that much more special.

I am standing behind Coach Wooden and between Michael Warren and Keith Erickson at the 2010 award dinner for the UCLA Anderson School of Management presentation of the John Wooden Global Leadership Award. I'd been invited to attend, and I happily accepted. I appreciated any opportunity to see Coach, in public or in private; he was always the rallying point to see old friends and to make new ones.

He had not been in great health, but he still had that gleam in his eye. He always made you feel you as if were the only person—even at an event like this award dinner where there were so many people pulling at him, vying for his attention. I wanted him to acknowledge me, but more so it was another opportunity for me to thank him. I wanted him to know that I was there for him, that it meant that much for me to be there and to support him and his family after all the support he had always given me. It was another occasion to celebrate his life.

I remember that I would often compliment Coach on his bolo tie, and once, at a basketball game at Pauley Pavilion, I met the son of an Indian chief who gave the Coach his bolos. I guess my compliments made an impression on Coach because he later surprised me with a bolo as a gift.

That was Coach Wooden, a man for others.

—Jamaal Wilkes

This is the last picture I ever took with Coach Wooden. It was snapped just prior to my introducing him that evening. It was an honor that I will forever cherish—although it almost didn't happen. Initially, I hesitated about agreeing to do the introduction because I didn't know if I could find the right words to describe how I felt about him. But I did know that if I didn't do it, I might deeply regret it later.

I agonized about what to say. I wanted to make it personal. I didn't want to recite statistics, because the John Wooden I knew was never interested in his own statistics. Instead, I wanted him to know the profound impact he'd had on my life. I wanted to thank him for his act of blind faith in offering me a scholarship based solely on the word of a friend. I wanted to apologize for not really caring about the Pyramid of Success when I was a youngster. I didn't have the personal depth to appreciate the jewels he offered me at such a young age. But later, as I raised my own family, the seeds he planted began to bear fruit as I heard myself reciting Coach's "two sets of threes" to my own children: "Never lie, never cheat, never steal; don't whine, don't complain, don't make excuses."

I wanted Coach to know just how grateful I was for the many conversations we had about life, about family, and about God; how much I appreciated our friendship, which became stronger over so many wonderful years; how playing basketball for him was one of my life's greatest joys.

Once onstage, Coach Wooden and I embraced, as we had done so many times in the past. But lately his embraces had felt different. When Coach was healthy and vibrant, his hugs felt as if he was holding me up, almost as if to say that he supported me. Now, I felt like I was holding him up, and I hoped he felt the same unwavering support from me.

Shortly after this picture was taken, I knelt down beside Coach. We held hands. I told him that I loved him, and he said he loved me, too. A look of serenity came across his face, and he smiled. I introduced him, and then he thanked me. I think I made him proud.

—Michael Warren

UCLAAnderson
School of Management
JOHN
WOODEN
GLOBAL
LEADERSHIP
AWARD

Following John Wooden's death on June 4, 2010, at the age of 99, his extended UCLA family turned out and transformed the Bruin Bear into a campus memorial.

Learn as if you were to live forever. Live as if you were to die tomorrow.

THE UNIVERSITY OF CALIFORNIA
LIGHT

EULOGY

Al Michaels

The following are comments delivered by Al Michaels, Master of Ceremonies at John Wooden's memorial service on June 26, 2010 in Pauley Pavilion.

John Wooden was, in the minds of many of us, the greatest coach in the history of sports. He pooh-poohed that, but I told him once, "Coach, you have only yourself to blame. You shouldn't have gone out and won those 10 national championships in 12 seasons. It's your fault."

The reason we're here today to celebrate and commemorate the life of Coach Wooden has only a little to do with the banners that ring the rafters of Pauley Pavilion. This day is about celebrating the life of a man who, over the course of almost a full century, personally touched, inspired, and enriched the lives of several thousand men and women, boys and girls. He was a man for all generations.

He was born when the automobile was just out of its infancy and the airplane was seven years old. And he lived to see men walk on the moon and to see computers recast the world. But he was never resistant. He understood how to shift with the times, and Coach Wooden was much too smart to step in front of an onrushing train.

Through it all, he never wavered from his core values. His life was built on an indestructible, unshakeable foundation. Over the last 10 years, or from the time John Wooden turned 90, many of us here today were with him when he would address students or other young people. And if there is one thing I will never forget, it was the look on the faces of almost every 14- or 16- or 18- or 20-year-old in the room when Coach spoke. They were simply enraptured. And that's why he was a man for all generations. He had a complete understanding of the art of communication. It reminded me of the old commercial: "When John Wooden talks, people listen." And they listened intently.

Pauley Pavilion has been the home of UCLA basketball for 45 years. It can be home for 100 more, and we'll never forget that Coach spent so many of those years after his retirement in his seat near the Bruins bench. A spotlight shines on this now because his spirit will be a part of this building forever.

And the court itself—initially Coach had no interest in the court being named after him, but finally after much prodding, he relented. But it was conditional. The court had to be named for his beloved Nell as well, and then he insisted that Nell's name come first. Doesn't that tell you something else about John Wooden: He was the classic gentleman—ladies first.

John Wooden had the ability to say more in one sentence than most of us could in one hour. My favorite Woodenism is "Never mistake activity for accomplishment." He touched the lives of tens of thousands of people directly and maybe millions indirectly. I think the luckiest, in addition to the family, are his former players. Bill Walton told me that when he visited Coach a couple of days before he passed, Coach looked at him and said, "I thought I was finished with you?" That was the Wooden sense of humor.

For so many of his players, John Wooden was a father figure. I had the great fortune to broadcast UCLA basketball on KTLA television over the course of Coach Wooden's last two seasons, and I think about one instance in 1974 when the Bruins had beaten Washington in Seattle on a Saturday night and the team had flown to Spokane on Sunday and bussed down to Pullman for a Monday-night game at Washington State. Coach had the bus stop at the Performing Arts Coliseum so the guys could get out and stretch their legs and go through a short practice. They practiced for about a half hour and then came back into the locker room. I was standing over in the corner. Coach looked at the team, and he talked about tomorrow's game, and he gave them the schedule, and then the last thing he said was "Now it's very cold and sleeting outside, so when you get out of the shower, I want you to dry your hair completely and thoroughly." I thought to myself, Not only is he their father, he is their mother, too.

There are many people in this building this morning that will tell you that John Wooden was the most remarkable man they had ever met. He was the complete man. And I look at this legacy and the 50 or so Wooden family members who are here, his son, Jim, and daughter, Nan, seven grandchildren, 13 great-grandchildren, and a great-great-grandchild on the way; this, too, is the legacy of Coach Wooden.

Today we celebrate a life of extraordinary accomplishment.

Emmy Award–winning sportscaster Al Michaels broadcast UCLA basketball games during John Wooden's final two seasons.

Coach Wooden's seat in Pauley Pavilion—Section 103B, Row 2, Seat 1.

Peden + Munk

U C L A BASKETBALL

John Wooden, Head Coach

Our chances of having a successful team may be in direct proportion to the ability of each player to live up to the following sets of suggestions:

1. Be a gentleman at all times.
2. Be a team player always.
3. Be on time whenever time is involved.
4. Be a good student in all subjects - not just in basketball.
5. Be enthusiastic, industrious, dependable, loyal, and cooperative.
6. Be in the best possible condition - physically, mentally, and morally.
7. Earn the right to be proud and confident.
8. Keep emotions under control without losing fight or aggressiveness.
9. Work constantly to improve without becoming satisfied.
10. Acquire peace of mind by becoming the best that you are capable of becoming.

* * * *

1. Never criticize, nag or razz a team mate.
2. Never miss or be late for any class or appointment.
3. Never be selfish, jealous, envious, or egotistical.
4. Never expect favors.
5. Never waste time.
6. Never alibi or make excuses.
7. Never require repeated criticism for the same mistake.
8. Never lose faith or patience.
9. Never grandstand, loaf, sulk, or boast.
10. Never have reason to be sorry afterwards.